THE HANOVERIAN KINGS AND THEIR HOMELAND

A Study of the Personal Union 1714-1837

THE HANOVERIAN KINGS AND THEIR HOMELAND

A Study of the Personal Union
1714-1837

Philip Konigs

The Book Guild Ltd.
Sussex, England

The Book Guild Ltd.
25 High Street,
Lewes, Sussex

First published 1993
© Philip Konigs 1993
Set in Baskerville

Typesetting by Robert C. Hawkins.
Horley, Surrey

Printed in Great Britain by
Antony Rowe Ltd.
Chippenham, Wiltshire.

A catalogue record for this book is available
from the British Library

ISBN 0 86332 756 7

CONTENTS

PREFACE

The Personal Union between Great Britain and Hanover was a factor in European politics for well over a hundred years. Yet only one book has ever been written about it, an edited version of a series of lectures held by an eminent historian who regretted that he had not been able to consult the Hanover archives. The probable reason why the subject has not been treated more often is an inherent difficulty: the main interest of the story lies in the way the foreign policies of the two countries were intertwined, but to describe these relations fully would amount to writing a diplomatic history of the eighteenth and early nineteenth centuries, an altogether different undertaking. Anyone who wishes to write about the Personal Union must often make unsatisfactory compromises between adhering to his or her theme and giving a sufficient explanation of the circumstances under which his or her personages were forced to act. This, apart from the obvious need for brevity, is why this book can only remain a study. In spite of its many imperfections, I believe its appearance is justified by the need to assemble some of the new facts that have come to light since my illustrious predecessor wrote his book nearly a hundred years ago. Having been fortunate enough to spend more time in both English and German archives than is usually available, I believe that I can contribute some of these facts myself.

Although I am proud of having a Scottish grandmother, I have sometimes used the words 'English' and 'England' where a Scotsman would have insisted on 'British' and 'Britain'. This was the general practice of the times, as it

7

unfortunately still is in most non-English-speaking countries.

All proper names have been spelt in the modern English fashion, as this seems to me the only method with any claim to consistency. Letters with diacritical signs such as the German 'ü' or the Scandinavian 'å' have generally been written in their simple form. In view of printing costs, I have tried to reduce the number of notes, but find it impossible to do without them altogether, if only to show that I have not invented any facts. Sometimes I have compromised by omitting notes where they seemed to be superfluous. Thus debates in Parliament will obviously be found in the Parliamentary History under the date mentioned in the text, reports by the Austrian ambassador in the Vienna archives shortly afterwards, etc. On occasion I have acknowledged my debt to an author only once, where several citations in short succession might have been called for.

My special thanks are due to my daughter Margaret (Mrs U. Weiss), my brother-in-law, K. Slatcher, and Dr J. Black of Durham University, who gave invaluable help in the editing and writing of the manuscript.

I

BRITAIN IN THE EIGHTEENTH CENTURY

During the closing years of the seventeenth century, the people of England had become aware that a great change was taking place in the fortunes of their country. In the past, England had been considered a medium-sized kingdom near the edge of the known world. Too weak to become a power on the Continent, and too strong to be invaded across the Channel, England had lived politically somewhat apart from the rest of Europe. She had been able to retain some institutions no longer fashionable in most other countries, and to develop them in her own way. Notable among these were an independent parliament with a not inconsiderable democratic element in its constitution, and the implementation of the Rule of Law, the concept that all authorities, including the king and his ministers, were subject to general principles of justice, including respect for the rights of the individual, and that the application of these principles could be enforced by the judiciary. But culturally and economically, England had remained an appendage of Europe, though contributing her share to the general development.

The discovery of America and of the sea route to India had given the English the opportunity of changing their situation. England now had direct access to the silks and spices of the Orient and to a source of raw materials across the Atlantic. As islanders, the English were accustomed to the sea and could readily expand their merchant marine and their fishing fleet to take advantage of the new conditions. After a slow start, they overtook their Spanish, Portuguese, and Dutch rivals, and became a nation of traders. England exported to all the world the products of her manufactures, among them woollen goods, pottery, furniture, and ironware of all kinds from stirrups to guns. She imported, partly for her own use, partly for re-export at a profit, tea, sugar, coffee, tobacco, spices, cotton, brandy, wines, and many other goods. The slave trade, i.e. the transportation of captured negroes from Africa to America, provided additional earnings. Trade had brought wealth, and wealth had brought power.

The extent of this power did not become apparent to Britain and to Europe until William of Orange became King of England, Scotland and Ireland in 1688. Unlike the preceding Stuarts, who had generally pursued a passive policy of friendship towards France, William led his kingdoms to take an active part in the fight to prevent French dominion over Europe. While the navy held down the French fleet, and British soldiers played a decisive role in land battles, Britain's gold helped her allies to keep on fighting. By the end of the War of the Spanish Succession (1714), Britain was acknowledged as the second power in Europe, a necessary component of any coalition capable of withstanding France, still the strongest country in Christendom.

As contemporaries kept reminding each other, Britain's position was founded on the wealth derived from her commerce, and for the entire eighteenth century and beyond the main object of British policy was the preservation of her trading status. In order to do this, three things were essential. First, a powerful navy must be maintained, not only to defend the island, but also to protect British merchantmen on the high seas and to blockade foreign ports if this became necessary. The army, on the other hand, tended to be neglected in peacetime. Second, the coast of the Continent across the North Sea must not fall into the hands of one great power. If such a power, say France, should ever control the Low Countries, that power could use the ports as bases to prey on English shipping and block English trade. It would then have the island at its mercy.

Third, it was vital to have a good supply of naval stores, such as masts, hemp, tar, etc. both for the navy and for merchant ships. These materials came from Russia and were brought to England either via the Baltic or, more rarely, round the North Cape. If the supply ever failed, British ships would be unable to leave port and trade would come to a standstill. Several times, efforts were made to obtain naval stores elsewhere, especially from North America, but results were always unsatisfactory.

Britain believed that it was desirable to have colonies. These were not great territories like the contemporary Spanish and Portuguese, or nineteenth-century colonial empires, but small sugar islands or fortified outposts where British traders and their goods would be safe from marauding tribesmen or local potentates anxious to replenish their war-chests. Such outposts might also serve as convenient bases for the navy. The exception to the rule was the east coast of North America, left unoccupied by the Spanish and settled mainly by enterprising individuals and private companies. At the beginning of the eighteenth century, America was treated chiefly as a convenient dumping-ground for adventurers, petty criminals, religious and political deviationists, and other social misfits. The real worth of these territories was only just becoming apparent.

The wealth accumulated by the English merchants (and their Scottish fellows after the Union of 1707) was not evenly distributed. The gap between rich and poor was enormous. But enough of the profit found its way downwards to make the lot of the lower classes much better than it had ever been before. Food was plentiful and cheap, especially because of the development of the Newfoundland fisheries. There was work for everyone willing to go where it was to be found. Opportunities for bettering the social position into which a man was born were not easy to find, but they were there. The nobility was not an exclusive class as it was on the Continent. Intermarriages between rich commoners and the heirs of noble titles were not rare, and the younger children of nobles did not inherit their fathers' rank and must descend to become commoners. On the whole, Britons were not dissatisfied with life as they found it. They were very proud of their new role in the world, which they ascribed to their innate superiority and the perfection of their constitution. The Glorious Revolution of 1688 was still fresh in their minds. Parliament and the nation had broken the bonds of tyranny, restored the ancient rights of Englishmen, and in the Bill of Rights formulated a system of government that would maintain their liberties for ever. Britons were free, members of other nations were slaves.

While the English of the time can thus be fairly described as self-satisfied and xenophobic, they were not insular in the sense of being ignorant of the world about them. They were already enjoying the benefits of a free press. After the government's attempt to maintain a censorship had been thwarted in 1697, a number of regular newsletters and newspapers had appeared which competed with each other to furnish their readers with as much information as possible. In addition there was a flood of pamphlets, mostly partisan and often virulent in tone, on the problems of the day. All these were widely circulated and perused by several readers in succession. It mattered little that literacy was not universal. Thousands of coffee houses in London and the provincial towns served as information centres and debating clubs. A patron who could read, felt both obliged and was delighted to read out the contents of a news-sheet to those who could not do it for themselves. Lengthy discussions often followed. Thus the English public were much better informed than their contemporaries on the Continent, who were — with the exception of the Dutch — generally restricted to newspapers published under the auspices of the local government, and containing mainly court news and a few other items of national and international news consider-ed to be good for the populace, or which could not be withheld.

As a consequence, a body of public opinion began to form and to make its influence felt, although in theory government was entirely in the hands of the king and his ministers. One forum from which public opinion could sway those in authority was Parliament. Although the right to vote was restricted, and many constituencies were under the control of powerful individuals who could appoint members of their choice, in others there was real competition, especially in the counties, where the average number of voters was 4000. In such constituencies, the vote would go to the men whose opinions tended to reflect those of the population in general. Even after they had been elected, many Members of Parliament felt free to change their mind on current issues. This was especially the case with the county members, mostly belonging to the lesser gentry, often with a long tradition of parliamentary service. They generally voted with the government of the day, but could be difficult when they thought ministers were acting tyrannically or paying too much attention to foreign interests. No government could afford to neglect these country gentlemen, whose attitudes were of course often the same as those of the public in general.

Another way for public opinion to put pressure on the king's ministers was through the mobs, especially, but not exclusively, those of London. Once the fury of the mob was aroused on some popular issue, there was hardly any way of restraining them. The police were few and badly organized, the army was small and could not be efficiently employed against widespread rioting. Mobs would smash windows, threaten the carriages and the very lives of unpopular figures, and set buildings on fire. The turmoil would go on until something was done to appease the populace. Mobs paid little regard to reason or questions of national policy. Thus, in 1757, in the midst of a war with France, mobs ran riot all over England, assaulting members of the gentry and threatening to burn down their houses because Parliament had passed a militia law with which they disagreed.[1]

Ministers also had to reckon with the influence — plutocratic rather than popular — of the rich traders and bankers of London and other cities. Trade being the life-blood of England, it was hard to resist their demands, especially if backed by bribes in the right places.

English society was permeated with violence. Life was short and liable to be terminated at any moment by diseases such as smallpox and consumption. It was therefore also cheap. Murders, highway robberies, and attacks by footpads were common. Harsh punishments for those who were caught, such as the mandatory death sentence for theft or poaching, did little to deter the criminals. While the majority of the population were pious and conservative, the more active, trendsetting Englishman of the times was distinguished by his total lack of inhibitions. Whatever activity he was engaged in — preaching, politicking, fighting, gambling, drinking, whoring, or thieving — he entered into it with a zest and a total disregard of consequences that may go far to explain Victorian prudery as a natural reaction. On the Continent, the English were regarded as rich, powerful, arrogant, eccentric, and more than a little uncouth.

☆ ☆ ☆

In the year 1700, when William of Orange was reigning as William III, William Duke of Gloucester, the future heir to the throne of England, died at the age of twelve. There were no other legitimate heirs, and neither King William or the next in line, Princess Anne, could be expected to have any more children. Anne's half-brother James, later to be called the Old Pretender, was excluded from the throne because he was a Catholic. William had to look for another successor. The nearest Protestant relatives of the Stuart dynasty were James I's granddaughter Sophia, dowager Electress of Hanover and her son George Louis, the reigning Elector. Few people in England had ever heard of Hanover or George Louis, and nobody wanted a foreigner as king, but there was no one else. The vast majority of the nation were not prepared to tolerate a Catholic king after their experience of James II. A republic was abhorrent to the people after the rule of Cromwell. There were indeed living descendants of Henry VII, who might have had a claim to the throne under Henry VIII's will, but they had become too insignificant to be considered.

So Parliament passed the Act of Settlement, assuring the succession to the Crown to Sophia and the heirs of her body. The occasion was used for a further affirmation of the liberties already embodied in the Bill of Rights and the imposition of additional restrictions on the Crown to prevent the repetition of certain actions of William III which had displeased the English. The act provided, *inter alia* that Britain was not to be involved in wars concerning the king's dominions in Germany without the express consent of Parliament; that no foreigner, even though naturalized, could be appointed to a post in government service; that no royal decree was valid unless countersigned by a member of the Privy Council; that the king was not permitted to leave his British dominions without previous consent of Parliament; and that the king did not have the power to pardon any of his ministers who might be impeached by Parliament. These were the conditions under which George Louis was to become King of Great Britain and Ireland.

A few months before William's death in 1702, Britain, the Netherlands and the German Empire (i.e. Austria and most of the German states) had begun the War of the Spanish Succession in order to prevent Louis XIV's second grandson Philip of Anjou from becoming King of Spain and thus threatening to unite France and Spain under one Crown. The allies' candidate for the Spanish throne was Charles of Habsburg, the Emperor's second son, who was believed to be acceptable to the Spaniards as a member of the dynasty which had hitherto ruled Spain. When France had been almost brought to her knees, but Spain had proved unconquerable, the British concluded the separate Peace of Utrecht (1713), in which Philip was acknowledged King of Spain against the solemn assurance that he would never become King of France. Britain withdrew her troops from the battlefield and left her confederates to fight on alone. This apparent desertion of her allies earned her the epithet of 'Perfidious Albion', a term of opprobrium that was to be used against Britain by her Continental enemies for the next two hundred years. However well this designation may have been deserved on other occasions, it was hardly so on this, for there had been a change in the political situation. After the deaths of his father and his brother, Charles had inherited the Austrian dominions in Germany and become Emperor. To make him King of Spain would have brought about the very thing Britain had entered the war to prevent: the union of two great Continental powers under one monarch. Nor did the Peace of Utrecht neglect Austria's interests, as she was awarded the Spanish possessions in Italy with the exception of Sicily which was given to Savoy. France was perhaps more justly accused of deserting her German allies, the Wittelsbach princes of Bavaria and Cologne, at Utrecht, but no derogatory epithet remained attached to her.

Charles, now the Emperor Charles VI, could not bring himself to give up his hopes of the Spanish throne, and continued the war, but soon saw that he had no hope of victory without British help. In the spring of 1714, he concluded the Peace of Rastatt, in which he obtained the Spanish Netherlands (modern Belgium), but had to restore conquered Bavaria and Cologne to the Wittelsbachs. From the beginning, the Hanoverian army had not fought with the other troops of the Emperor, but had joined the British in Flanders. Both allies had acquired a high regard for each other, and the soldiers had parted with mutual regret when Britain made peace. George Louis decided to continue fighting both because of his attachment to the Emperor and a fear that a revived France might aid the Stuarts and prevent him from obtaining the British throne. He made peace together with the Emperor, but he would never forgive the British ministers responsible for the Peace of Utrecht.[2]

2

THE ELECTORATE OF HANOVER

The House of Hanover (properly Brunswick-Luneburg) is a
branch of the Guelf family, one of the oldest princely houses
in Europe, tracing its descent in an unbroken male line
from ancestors living at the time of Charlemagne. The hero
of the Guelfs was Henry the Lion, who in the twelfth
century had fought and almost beaten the Emperor
Frederick Barbarossa. After finally being defeated, Henry
was despoiled of his great fiefs, the dukedoms of Saxony and
Bavaria. All that was left to his heirs was his personal
inheritance, the Duchy of Brunswick, i.e. part of the Harz
mountains and the territory to their north as far as
Luneburg. Under his successors, this duchy was split up
until at one time there were more than half a dozen tiny
duchies scattered across the land, each with a share in the
rich mines of the Harz, though the family continued to
maintain a sort of unity and a common policy. During the
seventeenth century, various family pacts were concluded
which served to bring the duchies together again. By 1706,
George Louis had succeeded in uniting all the Guelf
territories under his sovereignty, with the exception of
Brunswick-Wolfenbuttel, held by an elder line. The Guelfs
were once more a power to be reckoned with.

The Guelf family had done poorly at the peace of
Westfalia, which ended the Thirty Years' War in 1648.
Owing to their weakness and a premature peace with the
Emperor, they had failed to obtain any of the rich

territorial prizes distributed among their neighbours, and had lost territories which had been ruled by Guelf princes for over a hundred years. Thus the adjacent ex-bishoprics of Minden and Halberstadt went to Brandenburg-Prussia, while those of Bremen and Verden were allotted to Sweden. All the Guelfs had been able to secure for themselves were the right to rule the Bishopric of Osnabruck in alternation with a Catholic bishop, and the right to protect the Protestants living in the ecclesiastical territory of Hildesheim, lying almost at the gates of Hanover city.

The new state brought together under the rule of George Louis was ambitious to increase its territory and had at the same time to protect itself against powerful neighbours with similar aims. To its east, the Electors of Brandenburg and Saxony were always on the lookout for territorial gains. To its north, Sweden occupied the duchies of Bremen and Verden, while Denmark also held large dominions in Germany and would dearly like to have controlled the mouth of the river Elbe. But the gravest threat to Hanover was felt to come from the west, where France was steadily encroaching on German territory and might soon become a neighbour too powerful to resist.

Hanover was a part of the Holy Roman Empire, a unique political entity described by Voltaire as being neither Holy, nor Roman, nor an Empire. While the first two parts of this gibe were indisputably correct, the same cannot be said of the third. True, the Emperors had not been able to establish their authority in the manner of the French or Spanish kings. They had been forced to grant important rights to the princes of Germany at the time of the Aurea Bulla (1356) and the peace of Westfalia (1648). The princes had obtained a considerable share in the imperial authority, and were independent in their own states, especially in administrative, financial and military matters. They were even permitted to form alliances with foreign powers and to wage war, but not against the Emperor or the Empire. Nor could they secede from the Empire. Although thus not truly sovereign, all princes with a vote at the Imperial Diet were considered to be sovereigns and their children were held to be of royal birth. For some reason this was accepted by the rest of Europe, and until its present-day demise, the royal marriage market was flooded with eligible, though often impecunious, German princes and princesses.

But considerable powers remained with the central authority. The Emperor was still the Liege Lord of Germany and had the sole right to promote princes in rank, to dispose of fiefs that had fallen vacant, to grant full rights to children of morganatic marriages, and similar privileges. The Empire could declare war in the name of its constituent territories, declare the ban of the Empire against recalcitrant princes, pardon offenders, and make laws, especially on penal and economic matters.

Some of these powers could be exercised by the Emperor alone, for some he needed the consent of the College of Electors, for others, the consent of the entire Diet. As the legal situation was never very clear and continually disputed by factional interests, there would often be difficulties and long delays which sometimes seemed to leave the Empire deadlocked, but were generally surmounted in the end. When Pufendorf, the eminent jurist, described the Empire as '*horribile aliquod corpus et monstro simile*', he was referring to the Empire's legal problems, and not to the Empire itself.

In practice, three things held the Empire together, namely, the fears of its component states, German patriotism, and the Imperial courts of law. First, while proudly maintaining their sovereignty and independence, most German princes were well aware that they would soon become the victims of predatory neighbours unless they remained under the protection of some stronger power. Only under the rule of an Emperor powerful enough to keep the peace within the Empire and ward off foreign invaders (but not strong enough to impose his will on a league of his subjects), did they feel safe. This is why the Head of the House of Austria was always — with one disastrous exception — elected as Emperor. Austria alone had sufficient force at its disposal to cow an errant prince into obedience, and only Austria could unite the weak and divided levies of the smaller states into a useful body of troops. Second, German patriotism, usually decried as a negligible factor, played an important part in the politics of the time. In spite of their loyalty to their local prince, all Germans were aware that they lived in a common Empire. Few people west of the Elbe dwelt more than a day's journey away from some imperial Free City. Prayers were regularly said for the Emperor throughout the land, both in Catholic and Protestant churches, and this was an age when everybody went to church. Germans, especially the educated classes, were deeply disturbed by the weakness of their country and longed for deliverance. Third, there were two central courts in the Empire. The Imperial Supreme Court (*Reichskammergericht*), founded in 1495 and finally resident at Wetzlar, was a court of appeal against the decisions of the tribunals of the states of the Empire, and its decrees could be enforced even against heads of state. This court maintained the unity of law in Germany, and was responsible for the general introduction of Roman law in the Empire. In later years, it was partly superseded by the Aulic Council (*Reichshofrat*) of Vienna. The Aulic Council was originally the Emperor's private court, instituted to assist him in his role as the supreme fountain-head of all justice. In time it expanded its jurisdiction while the court at Wetzlar was hampered by lack of funds and personnel.

In spite of its many shortcomings, the Empire worked fairly well and managed to fulfil its task of keeping Germany united and free of foreign occupation — until a power arose that felt strong enough to upset the balance. Of course the Empire's path was not an easy one. Although no single state could attack its neighbours without drawing the Emperor's wrath upon itself, there were still opportunities for expansion. One of these could be a war in which a foreign power was involved, and the allies of the victor could claim some advantage for themselves in the peace treaty, another was a disputed inheritance. In this way the Guelfs had acquired the duchy of Lauenburg (south-east of Hamburg). When the last duke died in 1689, and while the Emperor was engaged in a war with France, George William of Celle had immediately occupied the duchy, although his right to do so was at the least doubtful, and fifty years later his heirs had to pay compensation to other claimants. The duchy remained in Guelf hands until 1815. A further opportunity for aggrandizement might arise during the interregnum following an Emperor's death, when the Empire was ruled by hereditary vicars. An enterprising prince, such as Frederick II of Prussia, could use this period of weakness to create a *fait accompli* which would be difficult to correct later on.

Because of the recurrent dangers threatening both from within and without the Empire, most major German princes had to keep strong forces under arms at an expense which often came near to overtaxing their resources. In times of peace, they were therefore quite willing to hire their troops out to someone who required their assistance. This arrangement provided training for the soldiers and much needed cash for the exchequer. Thus Hanoverians in Venetian pay had fought against the Turks in the Peleponnese during the second half of the seventeenth century.

When the Turks had besieged Vienna in 1683, and during the following war, George Louis's father Ernest Augustus had given valuable assistance to the House of Habsburg, and had asked to be advanced to the rank of Elector as a reward. The Emperor could hardly refuse, and he also felt that the Rhenish Electors (Cologne, Trier, Mainz, and the Palatinate) were coming too much under the influence of France, and a counterweight was needed. Ernest Augustus was further aided by the Elector of Brandenburg-Prussia for the same reason, and because Brandenburg wanted a second Protestant to replace the Elector of Saxony, who had become a Catholic. So Ernest Augustus was invested with the Elector's hat, and attained the highest dignity the most populous country in Europe could confer. The Elector of Hanover was thus not the petty German princeling his Jacobite detractors made him out to be, but a high-ranking prince of the Holy Roman Empire with influence both inside and outside Germany.

The population of Hanover was estimated at about 800000 in 1740, and was perhaps a little over 600000 in 1714, while Britain, with Ireland, had somewhat over 8 million inhabitants. The majority of the people were peasants farming the richer lands of a still underpopulated country. Agriculture was as yet unspecialized, but was profitable enough for many farmers to rise above the bare subsistence level. Most of them lived under some variety of the so-called *Meierei-Verfassung*, a system of hereditary tenure which gave the farmer a right to the land possessed by his father, provided he paid certain dues and rendered certain services stipulated in his contract, obligations which could not be increased by the landowner. The farmers thus felt safe on their own land, and in this way were better off than many of their fellows in other states of Germany. Besides the dues and services owed to his landlord, the peasant also had to pay taxes to the government at rates determined by the Diets of the various duchies into which the country had been divided. These taxes were, however, relatively light because the Elector had an independent source of income from the mines of the Harz mountains. In his report of 1708[1] the English envoy to Hanover estimated that about half the income of the Electorate came from the Harz mines. Without taxing his subjects unduly, the Elector was able to keep up a splendid court which aroused the admiration of visitors.

Three-quarters of a century before George I became King of England the Guelf duchies had suffered grievously during the Thirty Years' War. The damage caused by the pillaging and requisitioning of the armies passing through the country was tremendous, and perhaps a third of the population had died in the fighting and through famine and pestilence. Nothing of this destruction was visible in the countryside in 1714. The ruins of the flimsy houses had long since crumbled to dust or been rebuilt, the deserted fields had reverted to woodland or were tilled again, and two new generations had grown up. But the proud independent spirit that had once characterized peasants and burghers had been broken. The common people were no longer of any account, even their ancient Low German language was no longer used in offices and courts, having been replaced by the more fashionable High German of Vienna. Under the Elector, the nobles ruled the land while the lower classes were kept out of politics. Only rarely is it possible to catch a glimpse of the feelings of the people before the end of the Napoleonic period. One example is the hero's welcome given to Frederick II of Prussia when he passed through Hanover after the Seven Years' War.

When George Louis heard that he was to become King of England, he did not regard the news as an unmixed blessing. He had visited England as a youth — one of the first to include London in his grand tour — and had not been favourably impressed. He had disliked the turbulence of the English and their lack of respect for the nobility. He knew that in 1649, only eleven years before he was born, the English had deposed and beheaded their anointed king after what must have appeared to him as a sacrilegious farce of a trial. In 1688, when George Louis was already a grown man, the English had deposed and exiled another legitimate king whose rule was not to their liking. Despite all protestations that he was the legitimate heir, he would owe his reign to an Act of Parliament, and his rule would be hedged about with restrictions incompatible with his ideas of royal dignity.

Even if George Louis saw his accession to the English throne as a duty rather than a pleasure, he can have been in no doubt whether to accept. He was the heir of an ancient line striving to regain its former greatness. His good neighbours, the Electors of Saxony and Brandenburg, were already Kings of Poland and in (not yet 'of') Prussia. His lands bordered on territories belonging to the Kings of Sweden and Denmark. Even the lowly Landgrave of Hesse to his south had a son and heir who was married to a Swedish princess and might one day become (as actually happened) King of Sweden. In such circumstances, the opportunity to become King of England, the second power in Europe, could not be turned down. Quite apart from his personal advancement, the union of the two crowns would immensely increase the power and prestige of his Electorate, which at that time was his chief concern. He might indeed have resigned the throne in favour of his brother Frederick, Bishop of Osnabruck, and later Duke of York, but Frederick was an amiable nonentity whose rule in England would not have benefitted the Electorate. Even worse, Frederick was childless, and after his death the succession to the English crown would have passed to the House of Brandenburg, something no Hanoverian could possibly permit.[2] (Frederick has but one claim to fame: he is the only tourist known to have returned from Venice complaining that the fair ladies of the sea-girt city were unapproachable.)

The Electress Sophia and George Louis informed the Emperor of their right to succeed to the English throne as soon as they had received the official notification,[3] but George Louis could not be persuaded to take any action beyond this. Though continually urged to do so by factions in England, by his mother, and by the great philosopher Leibniz who lived at his court, he refused to intervene in English politics to ensure his succession. As he explained to his envoy to Vienna,[4] no party in England openly favoured the Pretender, but there might be people who disguised their intentions. It was better to keep quiet until his opponents made their intentions clear, and then discredit them before the nation. When even the Emperor was becoming uneasy about George Louis's inaction — the Emperor did not want Britain to fall into the hands of a puppet of France — he wrote a second similar letter of assurance to his envoy. This wait-and-see policy was certainly successful, and may have been the only safe one. An active promotion of the Hanoverian cause might well have increased unrest in England, brought forth counterpropaganda by the Jacobites, and endangered the succession. It would certainly have disturbed Queen Anne, whose health was poor, and who did not like the prospect of being succeeded by the Electress Sophia, a woman older than herself.

George Louis had led an active life. As a prince, he had commanded the Hanoverian troops at the relief of Vienna in 1683, and had taken part in three battles afterwards, seeing two of his brothers killed in action. During the War of the Spanish Succession, when he had already succeeded his father as Elector, he was appointed commander-in-chief of the Imperial army on the Upper Rhine, partly because Queen Anne had urged him to take up this post. But he had found himself unable to do anything. The corps he commanded, a miscellaneous collection of troops from the smaller states of the Empire, was poorly trained, far below strength, and of little use in the field. Furthermore, his colleague Prince Eugene of Savoy, soon moved off to the Netherlands to cooperate with the Duke of Marlborough. After two frustrating years, George Louis resigned the command of this 'shit of an army', as he called it, and returned to Hanover. He did, however, earn one reward from his period as general. The College of Electors, which had formerly refused to admit the Emperor's new appointee to its councils, now gave up its objections, and George Louis was universally acknowledged as Elector.

The news that the court of Hanover received from England after 1712 was disquieting. The hitherto ruling Whigs had been displaced from the government by the Tories under the leadership of the Earl of Oxford and Viscount Bolingbroke, both newly created peers. It was rumoured that they were trying to prevent the Hanoverian succession and have the son of James II raised to the throne as James III. These rumours were not unfounded. Oxford and Bolingbroke were indeed attempting to ensure that James would inherit Queen Anne's kingdoms after her death, but only if he became a Protestant. If this was treason in Hanoverian eyes, it was hardly so in English ones. There is no doubt that a Protestant Stuart would have been much more welcome on the throne of Britain than an unknown prince from Germany. Although James had no more British blood than George Louis — his only British great-grandparent being James I, who was also the great-grandfather of George Louis — he belonged to the male line, was descended from English kings, and had been brought up to speak English. He was thus infinitely preferable to George Louis, who was a total stranger. However, when James, in March 1714, definitely refused to give up his religion, Oxford and Bolingbroke deserted his party and began to work for the Hanoverian succession, knowing that the nation would never accept a Catholic king. The change came too late to mend their personal fortunes.

When news of the Tory government's negotiations with the Pretender leaked out, the public became alarmed. In February 1714, there was a run on the bank which was only halted by a personal message from the Queen.[5] Shortly afterwards, motions to declare the Protestant succession in danger were defeated by only narrow majorities in both Houses of Parliament. The Whigs began to fear that their hopes of returning to office would be disappointed. They fed George Louis and his representatives with rumours about Jacobite plots and the gathering of armies in France, and asked that a member of the House of Hanover should come to England in order to be able to take charge of affairs immediately after the Queen's death. Finally even George Louis became worried. In March 1714, Schutz, his minister in London, asked the Lord Chancellor for a writ inviting prince George Augustus (the future George II) to take his seat in the House of Lords as Duke of Cambridge. The instruction for the minister was signed by the Electress Sophia, but it is probable that George Louis knew about it, although he later denied all knowledge.[6] The writ was duly issued, but at the same time the Queen informed Schutz of her extreme displeasure at the prospect of seeing a Hanoverian prince in England. She wrote three letters to Sophia, George Louis and George Augustus, assuring them of her friendship for the House of Hanover and explaining that the presence of a member of the House in London would not calm the discussion, but would raise doubts on her sincerity about the succession, and serve to support a party inimical to the Crown. She wanted to enjoy her kingdoms in peace until she died. These letters have been called 'the angry letters', and her refusal to invite George Augustus to London has been attributed to her reluctance to have a successor at her court and see 'her coffin before her eyes', as she described it. While these feelings doubtless had an influence on her decision, there is much to be said for the Queen's explanation of her attitude. Anne was perhaps not remarkable for her intelligence, but she knew England and the English well. She remembered that in her own youth the politicians who opposed William III had gathered round her, and she feared that something similar might happen again. The history of the following three reigns, when a nucleus of opposition always formed round the heir apparent, shows that her fears were not unfounded. But she did what she could to show that her refusal to invite George Augustus did not mean she had changed her mind about the succession. As a proof of her sincerity, she sent the Earl of Clarendon to Hanover with instructions to explain her position to the Elector personally.[7]

Only a few days after Anne had sent off her three letters, the Hanoverian Resident — Schutz had been recalled — presented a memorandum drawn up by Sophia and George Louis in response to an earlier request by the Queen to be informed of their wishes. Among other things, the memorandum requested permission for a member of the Electoral House to reside in England. Anne did not lose her patience, but answered in the same vein as before.[8] George did not reply, for shortly afterwards the Queen died and he was King of Great Britain as George I, his mother having fallen victim to a stroke a few weeks earlier.

When he received news of his accession, George did not set out for England immediately, although he was urged to do so by the Council of Regency and his minister in London, who were both afraid of a Jacobite rebellion. He let nearly a month pass before beginning his journey. The delay is usually attributed to his teutonic slowness and stolidity, but this explanation is unlikely to be correct. George had had considerable military experience and was quite used to quick decisions. Moreover, Queen Anne's death had been expected for some time. It seems more likely that he was waiting to see whether the Pretender would declare himself a Protestant and forestall him on the throne. Religious conversions for political reasons were not uncommon at the time. Thus the Elector of Saxony had become a Catholic in order to be eligible for the crown of Poland, and even one of George's own brothers had converted in order to further his prospects in the Imperial service. Not being a particularly religious man himself, George must have expected James Stuart to act similarly. The little Elector of Hanover would indeed have become the laughing-stock of all Europe if he had set out to become King of Britain and had found the throne occupied by another, whom everyone would consider its rightful owner. When it became clear that the Pretender would not move, George was ready to travel.[9]

3

GEORGE I AND THE GREAT
NORTHERN WAR

George I arrived at Greenwich on 11 November 1714,
greeted by a fleet of ships and boats filled with people who
wanted to see their new sovereign. Nearly all the nobles of
the realm were present when he landed, even Oxford and
Bolingbroke, though the King paid no attention to them.
He had intended to leave for London at 8 o'clock the next
morning, but could not set out before 11 o'clock, as time
was needed to arrange the cortège of 300 carriages which
preceded him. On eighteenth-century roads, the dust and
stench at the end of this long procession must have been
well-nigh intolerable, but no contemporary seems to have
thought this worth mentioning. Everywhere along the route,
he was cheered by the assembled crowds. In London, the
whole city was illuminated, and the guns of the tower were
fired in his honour. The devil, the pope, and the Pretender
were burnt in effigy many times over. Long after dark, the
King arrived at his palace of St James, where he took up
residence.

George travelled in the company of his Hanoverian
minister, Count Bernstorff, and of two ladies, the Countess
von Schulenburg and Frau von Kielmannsegge. His wife
had been left behind. Years before, after she had requited
his many infidelities in kind, George had obtained a divorce
and banished her to the lonely castle of Ahlden, where she
was to spend the rest of her life without ever seeing him or

her son (the future George II) again. Melusine von Schulenburg was certainly his mistress, Frau von Kielmannsegge probably was not, though everybody in England thought she was. She may have been his half-sister, being the daughter of a lady with whom his father had had intimate relations.[1] George was later followed by other Hanoverian ministers and a retinue of servants, altogether perhaps a hundred.

All contemporary sources agree that George was cold by nature and had few friends, though he was also just and had a high sense of duty. His distaste for court ceremonial was quite remarkable for an eighteenth-century monarch. He had asked that all ceremony on his arrival in London be omitted, and even left a will ordering that all pomp at his funeral should be avoided. As king, when he could not escape the traditional levee, he only appeared fully clothed, preferring to be dressed by his Turkish bodyservants Mohamed and Mustafa, instead of the Lords of the Bedchamber, to whom this duty should have fallen. Like a true German prince of his time, he had no regard at all for the wishes of the populace, and soon earned the dislike of his new subjects by refusing to show himself to the people from time to time and to receive their homage, as an English king was expected to do.

He could, however, unbend when he had to. The Austrian Resident Hoffmann reports that in June 1715, when the Jacobite rebellion was threatening, and his ministers urged him to court popularity, he mounted his horse and rode to Hampton Court, allowing his hand to be kissed and talking to the people. He ought to have done this long before, adds the good Austrian. When there had been an unfavourable public reaction to his attending the Lutheran service at Christmas in 1714, he visited the Anglican chapel the following Easter.[2] In later years, when he was quarrelling with his son, he often dined in public. But he gave up this practice immediately when it was no longer necessary, preferring to dine alone with his beloved Melusine von Schulenburg or a few intimates.

The old story that George never bothered to learn English is no longer believed.[3] In fact, he seems to have understood English quite well. He loved to go to the opera and the theatre, and while some plays may have been in French, his favourite play, Shakespeare's Henry VIII, must have been given in English.[4] But having learned English late in life and by eighteenth-century methods, his accent (quite likely more French than German) must have been very marked. This is borne out by the *Parliamentary History*, which notes that at the opening session of his first Parliament, he spoke a few words in English before asking the Lord Chancellor to read his official speech. He acted similarly when announcing the Jacobite rebellion in July 1715. If Parliament was too surprised and awed to react on these occasions, or members did not even understand what was going on, this was not so when the King tried to repeat his performance at the end of the session. No imagination is required to picture how the honest country squires received George's highly personal version of the King's English. Apparently he broke off his speech before he had finished, for this is the only time his words were not put on record. George never opened his mouth in Parliament again, except on three significant occasions. The first of these was at the end of the session during which Shippen, the notorious Jacobite, had made his famous remark that 'it is the only infelicity of His Majesty's reign that he is unacquainted with our language and constitution.' Shippen was sent to the Tower for these words, but the King evidently felt it necessary to show that he could indeed speak English. Similarly, he spoke a few words at the beginning and the end of the first session of his second Parliament. The reason can only have been the need to show any new members that he could speak their tongue. This fear of being laughed at in public may have led to the legend that he could not speak English at all.

The British constitution was still at an early stage of its development. The King was not only in theory, but to a large extent in practice, the head of government. All decisions were made in his name, and the final responsibility was always his. The old Privy Council which used to advise the monarch had become too large and unwieldy and had been effectively replaced by a cabinet consisting of the chief ministers, but as yet without a prime minister. Foreign affairs were administered by two Secretaries of State, one of whom, the Secretary for the North, was responsible for relations with all countries east of the straits of Dover including Austria, while the other, the Secretary of State for the South, looked after relations with France and the Mediterranean countries. In addition, both Secretaries had to attend to a number of internal affairs. The two Secretaries were supposed to work in harmony with each other, a pious aim that was usually only achieved when one of them was able to establish a strong ascendancy over his colleague, or eventually a powerful prime minister controlled them both. At other times British foreign policy sometimes seemed to be heading in different directions. This cumbersome arrangement lasted until 1782, when a single Foreign Secretary was appointed.

When he was still only Elector of Hanover, George had been supplied with plenty of information about England by his representatives in London and from various other sources, some of the latter of very doubtful value. One would have expected that he was at least moderately well prepared for his new role. But it is difficult to pass over the Earl of Clarendon's report on his visit to Hanover in 1714 (see Chapter 2). After several hours' conversation with George Louis, Clarendon wrote home that: 'It is very plain to me that he knows very little about our constitution.' Clarendon was a friend of Bolingbroke and must have known that the government had given up all hope of a Stuart succession. He was therefore unlikely to give an intentionally unfavourable picture of his future king. Clarendon's judgement is borne out by the fact that at his first Hanoverian council after his accession, George declared his intention to return to Hanover after a few months' stay in England and leave the government of that country to the Prince of Wales. Had he known anything about English politics, he would have realized that it would be impossible to carry out this intention. Probably George had read all the papers submitted to him and quite rightly remained sceptical, suspecting that everything had been written from some party standpoint, and that he would have to see for himself.

Whatever George may or may not have known about the English constitution, there was one thing he did not know, and that even the first three of his successors had to find out for themselves: he was not free in the choice of his ministers. The Act of Settlement had ensured that members of the government were answerable not only to the sovereign, but also to Parliament. As British ministers never seemed to tire of telling foreign visitors, their heads could roll on Tower Hill if Parliament found them guilty of treasonable activities. The King would be unable to pardon them. No British minister could dare to accept office unless he was sure of Parliamentary support.

The first weeks of the new reign were busy ones. George was continually besieged by politicians and noblemen who wanted a place for themselves or their relatives and protégés. The Austrian Resident complained to his government that the foreign envoys could not be presented to the King because he could find no time for them. English and German ministers could use the back stairs to gain access to the royal closet while this route was closed to diplomats.

The King's first act was to form a government. He had dismissed all Queen Anne's ministers immediately after his accession. They had been responsible for the Treaty of Utrecht, and their loyalty was suspect anyway. He had originally planned to appoint a ministry of national unity containing members of all parties, but he had to rely on the advice of the Whigs, the only friends he could be sure of, and they insisted on occupying all the important ministries. The few Tories who were invited to join declined to take up only minor posts, and a purely Whig government took office. The chief members of the new ministry were Townshend, Secretary for the North, Stanhope, Secretary for the South, Sunderland, and Walpole, the last still a rising star.

Still a stranger to his new country, the King believed he could not do without the advice of his faithful Hanoverians. Though the Act of Settlement did not allow him to appoint them as ministers, he could consult as widely as he chose. Already under Queen Anne, it had become usual for important decisions to be taken by an inner council of only a few men, instead of the full cabinet. Continuing this practice, questions of foreign policy were now discussed at meetings between Townshend, Stanhope, Bernstorff, and Bothmer before being submitted to the cabinet.[5] The English ministers did not yet object to this German participation in British affairs because their offices depended on the king's good will, and they were anxious to please. There were, however, some early signs that this state of affairs would not last. During the first months of the reign, the Hanoverians had had considerable influence on the distribution of posts, and had been well paid for their efforts, as was the custom of the times. But patronage was an indispensable instrument for British ministers, who could not control Parliament unless they were able to satisfy at least some of the wishes of the more influential members, and the Hanoverians soon had to leave this business to them. In September 1715, Townshend insisted that letters from the Emperor to the King on British concerns be written not in German, but in Latin. The Hanoverian ministers approved this step 'in order not to give the English grounds for jealousy'. However, added the Austrian Resident in his report to Vienna, in matters of the strictest confidence, letters to the king could still be written in German.[6]

The most important of the German ministers was Count Bernstorff, an old servant of the family whom George Louis had taken over when the Duchy of Celle was joined to Hanover in 1705. Bernstorff is unanimously described as a highly intelligent and loyal man, but of a rigid and unbending disposition, a quality which was becoming more pronounced now that he was growing old. Another important minister was von Bothmer, who had been George Louis's envoy to London until 1711, but had had to leave under a cloud because he had interfered too much in internal politics. He had returned a few months before George's accession, and was invaluable to the King because he knew England well and could speak fluent English. There was also Robethon, a French Huguenot refugee who had been private secretary to William III, had later taken service with the Guelfs, and had returned to England with George. A somewhat shadowy figure, Robethon was considered by contemporaries to be an *éminence grise*, but is now thought to have been not much more than a faithful servant, and a moderating influence on his immediate superior, Bernstorff. Hattorf, who was later to be Hanoverian minister in London for many years, still played a minor role. The large retinue of lesser servants George had brought over from Hanover soon diminished in numbers, chiefly because the King had to pay them out of his own pocket. The Act of Settlement did not permit them to be paid out of the English establishment, though the Attorney General had ruled that they could be furnished with food, candles and firewood free of charge.

☆   ☆   ☆

At the beginning of his reign, George was still very much more a German Elector than a British king. If he could use his new power on behalf of his Electoral dominions, he would not hesitate to do so. A suitable opportunity was at hand. Since 1701, the nations surrounding the Baltic Sea had been fighting in the Great Northern War. In that year, Denmark, Poland, and Russia had combined to despoil the young Charles XII of Sweden of his inheritance and regain territories lost in the course of the previous century. Charles had easily beaten back his enemies and forced Denmark and Poland to make peace, but had suffered severe defeat when he advanced into Russia and lost the Battle of Poltava in 1709. From then on Sweden had to fight on the defensive, especially as Denmark and Poland had recommenced hostilities.

The Electorate of Hanover had at first favoured the Swedes. Though it badly wanted the duchies of Bremen and Verden, which had become Swedish in 1648, for itself, it was preferable to have these territories ruled by Sweden, for whom they were only a distant outpost. If they fell into the hands of Denmark, to whose German territories they were contiguous, Denmark might use them to block Germany's outlet to the sea and establish a North German empire for herself. When in 1712, Danish troops began to occupy the duchies as Swedish territory, George Louis, with the connivance of the Swedish governor, had marched his own army into Verden and part of Bremen, ostensibly to provide a cordon sanitaire against the plague carried by the Danes. But he had not been able to forestall the Danish occupation of the important fortress of Stade on the river Elbe, considered to be the key to both provinces.

After Poltava, the Russians had overrun the Swedish provinces of Estonia and Livonia and taken the towns of Reval and Riga, the ports from which most of Britain's (and Holland's) naval supplies came. The Swedes had retaliated against Russia by placing an embargo on all shipping to and from the ports formerly in their possession. This embargo was enforced more and more strictly. A number of British ships were captured, and the supplies needed for both the royal and the merchant navy were in danger. Then, on 17 February 1715, Charles issued an edict which gave a completely free hand to Swedish privateers and made the Baltic too dangerous for British ships to enter. Clearly something had to be done if Britain's trade, her source of wealth and power, was not to come to a standstill through lack of naval stores.

Already under Queen Anne's Government, three or four ships of the line had been dispatched to the Baltic in order to protect British merchantmen, but this force had proved too weak to pass the Sound against Swedish opposition. Britain did not want to go to war with Sweden, not only because this would have made Russia the only power in the Baltic and given her a monopoly (the old Swedish monopoly had been eroded by sending ships to Archangel), but also because of a treaty of friendship concluded in 1700, and because of popular feeling in favour of one of the few Protestant powers. But Sweden could not be permitted to halt British shipping. A solution to the problem was found by sending a squadron of twenty ships of the line under admiral Sir John Norris to the Baltic, where he was to be joined by twelve ships from the Netherlands. The combined fleet would escort the British and Dutch merchantmen to their destinations, and on their return with the precious naval stores. It has often been suggested, even by contemporaries, that Norris was sent to further Hanoverian rather than British interests.[7] That this cannot be true is shown by the participation of the Dutch, who would never have sent their ships to aid the House of Hanover. But even if the navy was sailing on a purely British errand, perhaps a way could be found to enlist it in the service of Hanover as well.

If Hanover wanted a share of the spoils after the defeat of Sweden, especially the two duchies of Bremen and Verden, she would have to enter the war. Negotiations were under way early in 1715 with Denmark, who was already fighting Sweden, and Prussia, who was about to do so. Both countries were ready to accept Hanoverian assistance, but they expected Hanover to send troops to take part in the siege of the port of Stralsund and the neighbouring island of Rugen, which they had planned for the coming campaign. This George was unwilling to concede. Instead, he instructed his Hanoverian ministers to point out to the Danes and Prussians that he was about to send twenty British men-of-war to the Baltic to further operations against Sweden. Was this not assistance of the greatest importance and sufficient to dispense him from sending a few thousand men to Pomerania?[8] This was enough to satisfy the Danes, who on 12 May signed a treaty in which they promised to hand over the duchies to Hanover against payment of 300000 Reichstalers and Hanover's undertaking to enter the war against Sweden. Hanover's part in the war was to be limited to an annual war contribution and the protection of Denmark against a possible (or imagined) attack from the south. George also promised his good offices as King of Great Britain for the payment of certain subsidies claimed by Denmark for her part in the War of the Spanish Succession. Denmark was prevailed upon to give up Bremen on such easy terms because of her fear of Charles XII, who had just returned from a lengthy exile in Turkey. The country was close to exhaustion after several years of fighting, and the prospect of British aid came as a great relief. The Danes' real aim in the war was the recovery of their ancient provinces of Skane, Halland and Blekinge (the southernmost part of modern Sweden). These provinces had formed part of their kingdom since its foundation six hundred years before, but had been taken from them by the Swedes in 1658. Their recovery seemed worth almost any sacrifice, much as Denmark would have liked to keep Bremen, the only territory she had acquired during the fighting.

Negotiations with Prussia were more difficult, because the Prussians insisted on knowing exactly what the British fleet was going to do in the Baltic. They wanted to have it clearly expressed in the treaty whether the navy would only protect merchant shipping, or assist in the siege of Stralsund and bombard the town.[9] The assurances given by George's Hanoverian ministers did not satisfy them. Seeing no other way out, George ordered his Electoral minister at the court of Berlin to inform the Prussian king that he gave his royal word that the British squadron would act in every way to assist the operations against Stralsund, though he was unable to give a written engagement to this effect, as this would have to pass through the hands of his British ministers.[10] This promise finally induced the Prussian king to sign a treaty on the same date as the Danes. Against Hanover's entry into the war and a guarantee for parts of western Pomerania recently occupied by her, Prussia undertook to cede a few small territories to Hanover and to employ her good offices for the cession of Bremen and Verden to the Electorate.

While George was certainly treading on very thin ice when he promised the aid of the British fleet to Denmark and Prussia, he was not necessarily lying or prejudicing British interests. As King of Great Britain he could, with some justification and the approval of his British ministers, issue orders to retaliate against Swedish shipping for their seizure of British ships in the past. He could even order his navy to blockade the Swedish fleet in its port of Karlskrona in order to prevent further attacks. He could hope that an armed struggle would ensue and the Swedish navy be crippled. Even if the Swedes were only kept out of the way while the siege of Stralsund was going on, this would provide very material assistance to his new Electoral allies. But there can be little doubt that all his measures were taken with the thought of the acquisition of Verden and Bremen uppermost in his mind.

Norris's orders from the admiralty stated that he was to protect British merchant ships, to retaliate against the Swedes if attacked, but not to cooperate with the Danes against Sweden. He was also to obey any further commands he might receive from His Majesty.[11] These commands, issued at about the same time, were to communicate with the British ministers at Stockholm and Stralsund, who were to press the Swedish king for reparation, and in the meantime to intercept and detain all Swedish ships.[12]

According to Bonet, the Prussian envoy, he received further verbal instructions from Bernstorff, who told him to keep the Swedish fleet bottled up in Karlskrona.[13] But Bonet was something of a rumour-monger and is not wholly to be trusted. The only evidence we have is a paper of 'Queries and Answers' in the British Library.[14] It is unsigned and the names of the participants are not given, but one of them can only have been Norris, while the other may have been Bernstorff. Norris was told that the best station for preventing the transport of Swedish forces into Germany was about the island of Bornholm or off the harbour of Karlskrona, but it was not certain whether these stations would be safe for the ships. As Norris had been provided with ammunition only for a peacetime expedition and no hospital ships, he was to obtain extra ammunition and hospital facilities from the Danes. He was further to protect the trade of Lubeck, Hamburg, Bremen, and perhaps Danzig. This may bear out Bonet's report, but some parts of the paper are not easy to explain. For instance, it is difficult to imagine Bernstorff, whose experience of the sea was limited to a single Channel crossing, telling a British admiral where to station his ships.

Norris arrived at the Sound on 10 June and entered the Baltic a few days later. He found no Swedish ships, as the King of Sweden had wisely ordered them to stay at home. It was impossible for him to blockade Karlskrona because the Dutch absolutely refused to take part, and he was too weak to undertake the blockade on his own, as the Danes had not been able to furnish the extra ammunition he had expected to obtain.[15] A battle under these circumstances would have put his squadron at a grave risk, and he knew that nothing would have delighted the Danes and Russians more than to see the Swedish and British fleets batter each other into helplessness, leaving the dominion of the Baltic to them. He decided to take his squadron to the eastern ports with the merchantmen.

Norris's departure put the Danes into a difficult situation as they had counted on the help of the British ships to protect the siege of Stralsund and Rugen. They had sent a fleet of flat-bottomed boats to attack the island's defences. The Swedes, now able to leave Karlskrona, bottled up this fleet and threatened to cut off its supplies, although they could not reach it in the shallow waters where it had taken refuge. Seeing no other way out, the Danes sent their own navy to attack the Swedes. The ensuing desperate battle was indecisive, and both combatants were obliged to return to port to refit. The siege could proceed unhindered until the Swedes would be able to put to sea again.

Frederick William of Prussia tried to move heaven and earth in order to get Norris to come to the aid of the Prussian and Danish troops. He wrote to George, to Norris, and even to the Hanoverian ministry.[16] His minister in London was ordered to complain to Bernstorff that Norris was doing nothing, that promises made to him by George's ministers had not been kept, that he could not be expected to go on fighting alone, and that he might have other thoughts.[17] But all his efforts were fruitless.

The Danes were in a position to put more effective pressure on George. They were still in possession of the duchy of Bremen, and were resolved not to part with it until they had received some real assistance. At first they claimed that certain rights of the Duke of Holstein had been affected by the Danish-Hanoverian treaty, and that he must be satisfied. George tried to counter this by ordering his envoy to Copenhagen to tell the Danes that Norris had orders not to do anything to help Denmark until the duchy had been handed over. This was dishonest, as George could give no such orders to Norris. The Danes were unimpressed, and George had to get round the problems by giving his solemn promise that he would give the Duke an indemnification equivalent to that to be given by the King of Denmark.[18] This promise committed George to nothing, but was enough to silence the Danes on that point. But they continued to make difficulties and now asserted that they had not received all the money due to them under the treaty of alliance. The King finally understood that Denmark would go on finding excuses, and that he would have to give her some effective assistance to enable her to take Stralsund. The only way he could do this was by using the British navy to support the siege. In August, Townshend signed an order to Norris instructing him to leave eight of his ships behind in the Baltic when he left for England with the merchantmen. The ships were to join the Danish fleet and act in concert with it. Norris was warned by Robethon to expect this order and told that the King desired him to obey it, 'His Majesty having that affair very much to heart'.[19]

Townshend's order speaks only of British interests, of the necessity to protect the supply of naval stores, and of the importance of reprisals against Sweden, but these were obviously pretexts. At this time of the year, after Norris's departure with his convoy, there were no British merchantmen in the Baltic, and no Swedish privateers out after them. There can be no doubt that by adding the eight ships to the Danish fleet George violated his coronation oath in order to benefit Hanover. As will be seen later, a strong case can be made out that the acquisition of Bremen and Verden by the Electorate was of advantage to Britain. But in the autumn of 1715, the risk of a war with Sweden, who might have sent troops to aid the Jacobite rebellion, far outweighed the possible benefit of seeing the duchies in friendly hands.

It is not difficult to understand George's position. He was still a stranger in a country he did not like, and which did not like him. The Jacobite rebellion against his rule had already begun, and he might have to return to Hanover very soon. How could he miss this opportunity to fulfil his dream of many years, extend his home territory by a third, and make Hanover one of the most powerful states in Germany? He failed in his duty as King of Great Britain, but surely his failure is pardonable. But why did Townshend sign the letter to Norris? He must have known that he might be accused of betraying British interests and that his life could be in danger if the matter were brought before Parliament. His defence that he was only carrying out the King's orders would be ignored. Until some proof is found, it seems reasonable to assume that he was put under intense pressure by Bernstorff, who may have told him that if Britain would do nothing at all for George as Elector, he could always return to Hanover and leave the island to its fate. This sort of reasoning would have forced Townshend's hand, for he knew that Britain could not do without George. If the King deserted in the face of the rebellion, the Pretender might well obtain the throne and the ensuing civil war would ruin the country.

The order to leave the eight ships behind in the Baltic was not sent directly to Norris, but to the Hanoverian envoy at Copenhagen, there being no British ambassador to Denmark at the time. The envoy, Puchler, was permitted to inform the Danes about the order, but he was strictly enjoined not to part with it until he had proof of a positive command from the Danish king to his officers in the duchies to withdraw from them 'without ado and without difficulties'.[20] The Danes were in great fear that Norris would sail back to England with his entire squadron and leave them to face the refitted Swedish navy alone. If the Swedes should win this time, Stralsund would be relieved, the Danish landing fleet and the troops would be in danger, and the whole course of the war would change. They felt that they had been deceived by Norris in the past and might be deceived again. They did their utmost to induce Puchler to hand over the order to them. After holding out for some time, Puchler, who was ill, could bear their complaints and recriminations no longer and let the Danes have the order without first receiving the guarantee for Bremen and Verden. For a moment all George's plans seemed in danger. But after some further haggling and the payment of the sums claimed by Denmark, the Danish army vacated the duchy and it was occupied by Hanover on 15 October. Perhaps the Danish decision was speeded up a bit by George's threats to use force if the Danish troops did not retire. As soon as the duchies were in her hands, Hanover declared war on Sweden.

Norris left the Sound for England on 10 October and arrived nine days later with his convoy of invaluable naval stores. The eight ships under their commander, Captain Hopson, joined the Danish fleet and sailed with them to Rugen. The Swedes did not dare to attack, but as soon as the combined fleet had returned to Copenhagen, news was received that the Swedes had left Karlskrona in order to relieve Stralsund and rescue their king, and the allies set sail for Rugen once more. But there was no battle, as a severe storm obliged both combatants to return to port.[21] Rugen was taken on 15 November, and Stralsund on 22 December, Charles XII escaping to Sweden in an open boat. By the latter date, Hopson had already left the scene of action, but there is no doubt that the presence of his ships gave material aid to the Danish-Prussian allies. He had enabled them to take Rugen, and Stralsund was untenable without the island. The British navy had been employed in the service of Hanover.

☆   ☆   ☆

The plan of campaign for the following year (1716) provided for a joint invasion of the Swedish mainland by a Danish-Russian army from Zeeland. For this, the Russians had to be ferried across the Baltic, where they would be exposed to attack by the Swedish fleet. The Danes did not feel strong enough to protect them. Russia had recently built up a fleet of her own, but the sailors lacked experience, and a naval battle against Sweden would be a risky thing. It was therefore hoped that Britain would once again provide assistance. But Britain was not ready to do so without first trying to come to an arrangement with the King of Sweden. Norris had again been sent to the Baltic and arrived there on 8 June with nineteen ships of the line. His instructions were to wait for an answer by the King of Sweden to a memorial containing proposals for an accommodation between Britain and Sweden under the condition that British shipping was allowed to pass through the Baltic unhindered. If the Swedish answer should prove satisfactory, Norris was to divert the Danes from their proposed landing in Skane and other attempts on Swedish territory.[22]

Charles XII, however, returned the memorial without having opened it. Norris thereupon divided his squadron, sending six of his ships together with the six ships the Dutch had sent this year to convoy the merchantmen to the eastern Baltic. With the rest he blockaded Karlskrona, assisted by the Danes. The Swedish fleet could not leave port, and the Russians were safely ferried to Zealand.

When all seemed ready for the invasion in September 1716, Tsar Peter, who had made several journeys to the Swedish coast in order to inspect the defences,[23] decided to call it off. He claimed that the coast was too well defended and the season too far advanced for any hope of victory. His decision came as a great shock to the Danes, who had pinned all their hopes on the success of the planned attack. Though they were not yet ready to admit it, even to themselves, they knew that their last chance of regaining Skane, Halland and Blekinge had disappeared. Furious, they published a declaration (on 10 October) in which they accused the Tsar of failing to keep his word, mentioning that Norris, under express orders from King George, had made every effort to change the Tsar's mind. This declaration was immediately printed in all the English newsletters, causing an enormous uproar in the public and considerable disquiet among the politicians.

The question now arose where the Russian troops were to spend the winter. They had come to Denmark from Mecklenburg, which they had reached by marching from their winter quarters in Poland across Prussian territory. This had caused great uneasiness in Hanover, partly because several of George's ministers, among them Bernstorff, possessed estates there. An even more important reason for concern was the presence of foreign troops on German soil, and the danger this entailed for the independence of the Electorate and the Empire.

The Duke of Mecklenburg (more exactly: Mecklenburg-Schwerin) was in difficulties. In the past, Mecklenburg had been kept under the thumb of Sweden, for whom the country served as a corridor between her various territories in Germany. While the Duke wished to set up a standing army to defend his country and enforce his authority at home, it was in Sweden's interest to keep the Duke powerless and to support the local nobles, who refused to pay the taxes needed by the Duke, insisting on their rights and liberties. One would like to sympathize with the Duke's desire to protect his territory and establish a strong government in accordance with the spirit of the times and the example of his neighbours. But Duke Leopold was a violent, unbalanced man who managed to antagonize everybody, including the Emperor, whom he had tried to trick into coming to his aid by professing a readiness to convert to the Catholic religion. Already twice divorced, he had managed to marry a niece of Peter the Great on 19 April 1716, though the reasons why Peter agreed to the marriage have never been quite clear. The most probable explanation is that at the time the Tsar was toying with the idea of establishing a route to the open sea for Russia via the Mecklenburg ports and an inland waterway to the river Elbe.[24]

The Hanoverians had felt relieved when the Russians had left Mecklenburg for Zealand, but their fears returned in full strength when the news arrived that the Tsar would not attack the Swedish mainland. In August, George had sent a Hanoverian general to Copenhagen to press for the invasion. This general, von Bothmer, now told the Russian Chancellor that the successful continuation of the war might be in danger if the Tsar's troops were to spend the winter in Mecklenburg or elsewhere in the Empire.[25] Orders were also sent to Polwarth, the new British ambassador to Denmark, and to Norris to persuade Peter not to let his soldiers winter in Mecklenburg.[26] Both men did their best, but could not achieve anything. The Danes absolutely refused to let the Russians stay in their country, but would do nothing to hinder their landing in Mecklenburg out of fear that they might change their mind about leaving Denmark.[27] The Tsar would keep his troops out of the Empire only if Britain would promise to send her fleet to assist his landing in Finland, proposed for 1717.[28]

Bernstorff was so perturbed at the prospect of the Russians passing the winter in Mecklenburg that he conceived the idea of crushing the Tsar by seizing his ships and even his person. Stanhope, who at the time was at Hanover with the King, was inclined to favour the plan, but was restrained by George, who told him to consult Townshend, who had remained in London, before giving orders to Norris.[29] Townshend was horrified. He pointed out that a breach with the Tsar would lead to a prohibition of British commerce in the Baltic. Naval stores would be cut off and it would be impossible to fit out a fleet: 'this Northern war has been managed so stupidly, it will be our ruin.' He advised George to make peace with Sweden, even if it would cost him some sacrifice. Two days later, his secretary Poyntz wrote to Stanhope that Townshend thought that the Tsar's present greatness was chiefly due to George's parsimony, and that the Electorate should raise or hire more troops. Bothmer, who had been left behind in London, also wrote that the ministry believed George should increase his forces in Germany and should seek an accommodation with the Tsar.[30] These suggestions were highly obnoxious to the King, and were to contribute to Townshend's downfall.

Townshend had made one concession: if the King of Denmark were to carry out Bernstorff's proposal, Norris could be given private orders to assist him under the pretence of defending Denmark. But the Danes had no intention of embroiling themselves with the Tsar, and Norris did not receive any orders to interfere with the transportation of the Russians. Their troops were taken to Mecklenburg, where they spent the winter, causing great suffering to the country. Most of the local gentry sought refuge in Hamburg or Hanover. Estates left alone by the Russians in an effort to retain some Anglo-Hanoverian goodwill — such as Bernstorff's — were sequestered by the Duke, who alleged that he had a right to do so because their owners had left the country.

The Tsar offered to evacuate Mecklenburg if he were promised the aid of the British fleet for the coming year,[31] but George was unable to give such a promise because his British ministers would never have agreed. He did his best to keep up pressure on Peter by telling him that an agreement was impossible while the Russian troops remained in Mecklenburg. The King even began to consult with Denmark about an alliance against Russia, and some progress was made. When the Russians tried to occupy the ex-Swedish port of Wismar, just taken by the Danish, Prussian, and Hanoverian troops, it was successfully defended with the help of admiral Byng, who had replaced Norris in 1717. An attack on Mecklenburg by Hanover and Denmark, which the Emperor was willing to assist, was under consideration. A rift had opened up between the allies. Prussia was inclined to favour the Russians because she feared that they might invade her territory.[32] Relations between Russia and Britain were not helped by the abortive treaty negotiations that were held in London during the spring. The Russians had wanted to conclude a political alliance, but the talks were broken off when the British insisted that a commercial treaty must be signed first.

In June 1717, to the great relief of the Hanoverians, the Tsar ordered his soldiers to evacuate Mecklenburg, leaving only 3000 men behind to protect the Duke. The reasons for which Peter gave this order have been much debated. At the time, he was staying in Paris, and it is not unlikely that the French Regent had some influence on his decision. France had long been a friend of Sweden, and had recently concluded an alliance with Britain, and may have used her good offices on their behalf. But this does not seem sufficient to explain the Tsar's action. He had come to Paris with the intention of concluding some sort of political agreement with France, but had been politely refused. Peter therefore had no particular reason to gratify the French, though it is not impossible that he may have made the concession in the hope that this would make the Regent more amenable to his wishes. It seems more probable that he was influenced by the situation in Mecklenburg. That country was completely exhausted and unable to support the Russians any longer.[33] Moreover Duke Leopold, on closer acquaintance, hardly seemed a reliable ally. Russia could not afford to maintain a distant and unprofitable outpost against attack.

For the next two years, the war continued without a decision. Because of the differences between Sweden's enemies, no concerted action could be agreed upon. The Dutch had sent no ships to the Baltic in 1717 because they were afraid that war might break out between Britain and Russia, but provided a small squadron in 1718, when the major part of the British navy was engaged in the Mediterranean. Both Britain-Hanover and Russia tried to negotiate peace with Sweden, but had to give up when Charles XII refused to part with any significant portion of his dominions.

The situation changed completely when Charles was killed in November 1718 while attacking a fortress in Norway, then a part of Denmark. Exhausted Sweden immediately began to treat for peace. She had the option of coming to terms with Russia, who would insist on the cession of all or most of the Swedish territories in the east, but might help her preserve her western provinces, or with the western allies, to whom she would have to give

Pomerania as well as Bremen and Verden, but who could perhaps help her to regain at least some of her Baltic possessions. On the whole, the western alternative seemed preferable, not only because Sweden had much closer cultural and religious ties with the west, but also because the country might be reduced to a condition of vassalage towards Russia if she made a separate peace with the Tsar.

In April 1719, a Hanoverian envoy arrived at Stockholm in order to negotiate a peace treaty between Sweden and Hanover. The Swedes told him that they were prepared to cede Bremen and Verden, but would only do so if Britain would help them against the Russians with her fleet, and pay them considerable subsidies.[34] As the Hanoverian was unable to give any promises regarding Britain, the negotiations continued without a result. They came to life again when Lord Carteret reached Stockholm on 11 July. Carteret's instructions were to conclude a treaty between Sweden, Britain, and Hanover, and to mediate between Sweden, Denmark, and Prussia. He was further to restore the freedom of British shipping and to restrict the Tsar's power in the Baltic. Carteret knew how much George I desired to obtain Bremen and Verden for Hanover, and made it clear to the Swedes from the beginning that 'the Electoral interests are inseparable from the Royal ones'.[35]

Only a few days after Carteret's arrival, the Russian fleet came to the vicinity of Stockholm and troops landed on the islands between the city and the sea. At this moment of extreme danger, a strong party in Sweden, headed by the Chancellor, favoured an immediate peace with Russia, while the Queen and her husband, the Crown Prince of Hesse, preferred an arrangement with Britain. But the only hope of preventing a Russian attack on the capital was the arrival of the British squadron which was waiting at Copenhagen under Norris. Carteret, without being authorized to do so, promised that the fleet would come, writing to Stanhope that 'if I had not done so ... the Tsar would have had his peace six days ago'.[36] At the same time, Carteret wrote to Norris, strongly suggesting that the admiral would act in the King's interest if he proceeded to Stockholm immediately.[37]

But Norris refused to sail without a specific order from

47

the King, and George was not yet ready. He was unsure of the political situation. If Britain were to make common cause with Sweden too soon, she might have to face a coalition of Russia, Denmark, and Prussia. The British squadron in the Baltic was too weak to overcome the combined Russian and Danish fleets, and Prussia could invade Hanover without difficulty if she sided with the Tsar. The King, who was staying at Hanover, twice sent an ambassador, Whitworth, to Berlin with instructions to conclude a treaty. After considerable difficulties, which he could never have surmounted without the help of the French ambassador,[38] Whitworth was successful. Against a guarantee of her conquests in Pomerania, Prussia promised to join the efforts for an early peace, and gave an assurance that she would never enter into any engagements with the Tsar that were prejudicial to the interests of the Empire. When Denmark showed no signs of belligerence, the danger was over, and Norris could be ordered to sail to Stockholm.

The agreement with Prussia had been strenuously opposed by Bernstorff, who saw Prussia as the arch-enemy of Hanover. He was overruled by the King, advised by Stanhope. George saw that the preservation of Sweden, the only country able to prevent the absolute domination of the Baltic by Russia, was essential for Britain, and that Hanoverian interests must take second place, especially since Bremen and Verden were already in her hands. He now felt secure on his royal throne and had truly become King of Great Britain. Bernstorff remained in favour, but was no longer consulted on British affairs.

Norris sailed from Copenhagen, having received some last-minute reinforcements. After a few days' stay off Hano, where he waited for the news that the Anglo-Swedish agreement had been signed, he proceeded to Stockholm. There was no battle. The mere news of the approach of the British fleet had caused the Russians to withdraw to the safety of their port of Reval. In the treaty between Britain and Sweden, both parties promised to restore their ancient friendship, and guaranteed the peace between Sweden and Hanover, concluded earlier. To his great disgust, Carteret had been forced to insist on the cession of Stettin and part of Pomerania to Prussia. But he absolutely refused to pass on a similar request in favour of Denmark, who wanted to keep Stralsund and Wismar.[39] The Swedes would have nothing to do with Denmark, and Carteret had already promised them that he would not mention the subject. All that could be done for Denmark was the insertion of a clause in the treaty that made British financial aid to Sweden conditional on the conclusion of a peace with Copenhagen. Stralsund and Wismar were returned to Sweden, and Denmark obtained nothing.

During the following two years, the British fleet tried to assist Sweden against Russia. But the big ships of the navy were powerless against the flat-bottomed boats the Russians operated in the narrow waters around the Aland Isles, while their main fleet remained safe under the guns of Reval. The Tsar ridiculed British sea-power, which he said could do nothing against his country. But he was careful not to enter into war with Britain because he needed British trade. He even published a proclamation to the British merchants in his dominions, declaring that His British Majesty had broken his agreement with Russia and come to an agreement with Sweden solely for the benefit of Hanover without any regard to the interests of the English nation. He would therefore continue to protect the English merchants as before.[40] Russia was a poor country and could not do without the income and the capital provided by the British traders.

British and French aid to Sweden could not be continued when the South Sea Bubble burst and Law's Mississippi scheme in France came to a similar disastrous end. Both countries had to repair their shattered finances and were unable to engage in Baltic affairs. Sweden was left to make what peace she could with Russia and had to give up all her Eastern territories except Finland at the peace of Nystad in 1721.

The question whether George I's policy during the Baltic war was damaging to British interests has been debated for centuries and will probably never be resolved.[41] While Britain was forced to act against Sweden in order to protect her vital naval supplies, she also wanted to preserve that country as an independent power. Sweden was important as a counterweight against Russia in the Baltic and as one of the few Protestant states in the Empire and in Europe at a time when a return of Catholic predominance was still to be feared. Hanover wanted to obtain Bremen and Verden, and preserve the integrity of the Empire. These aims were not irreconcilable, and they were achieved. On the other hand, Britain under a native king would certainly not have aided the siege of Stralsund, and she might have reached an earlier understanding with Sweden if her policies had not been encumbered by the Hanoverian connection. If overmuch regard for Hanover caused a breach with Russia, it was not permanent. Although some years were yet to pass, Russia concluded a trade agreement with Britain, the only western country with which she did so before 1787. The agreement remained in force for fifty years, to the mutual satisfaction of both sides.

The Great Northern War was not popular in Britain. The Baltic was far away, and once attacks on British shipping had ceased, people thought only of the heavy taxes that were required for the annual naval expeditions. Sailors intensely disliked manning the Royal Navy ships in the Baltic, and the press-gangs had to be used, angering not only the seamen, but the politically far more important merchants who employed their services.[42] Opponents of the dynasty claimed that the war had nothing to do with Britain and was conducted for the benefit of Hanover, and many believed them.

4

EUROPEAN POLICY UNDER GEORGE I — THE END OF HANOVERIAN INFLUENCE

When George I ascended the throne, Britain was politically isolated. Her old friends, especially Austria, were still irritated at what they considered Britain's desertion of them at the peace of Utrecht, while relations with her former enemies, France and Spain, were still strained. Her only ally, the Netherlands, was too weak after the long wars with Louis XIV to be of any weight in international affairs. A renewal of the War of the Spanish Succession was out of the question. Even if Britain's land forces had not been reduced to a fifth of their strength in accordance with the old English prejudice against a standing army, the military situation had changed, and victory could not be hoped for. It was necessary to assure Britain's standing in the world by improving foreign relations. The ministry's first success, after a commercial treaty with Spain, was a renewal of the ancient friendship with the Emperor, arranged by Stanhope, who was personally acquainted with Charles VI from the time of the war in Spain. In the treaty of Westminster, concluded in the spring of 1716, the Emperor guaranteed the Protestant succession in exchange for British commitments in the Mediterranean. In the autumn of the same year, an alliance was concluded with Britain's ancient enemy France, an accord made possible by the need of the Duke of Orleans, who had become Regent after the death of Louis XIV, to protect his rule against the ambitions of

Louis's grandson Philip V of Spain. The crowning achievement was the Quadruple Alliance of 1718 (misnamed because the Dutch never joined) between Britain, France, and Austria. Peace in Europe seemed to be assured.

The Jacobite rebellion in 1715 was far more dangerous than is generally assumed today. Because its own forces were too weak to subdue the rebels, the government had to call in allies from abroad. The ministry decided to ask for troops from the Netherlands, who were obliged by treaty to defend the Hanoverian succession. It might have seemed natural to bring over Hanoverian soldiers to aid their monarch, but the presence of soldiers who owned their sole allegiance to the foreign-born king might have driven at least some of George's vacillating adherents into the arms of the Pretender. Instead, Hanoverian and other German troops were sent to Holland to replace the Dutch regiments fighting in Britan.[1]

The failure of the rebellion showed Europe that George I was safe on his throne, and convinced them that Britain was under a stable and reliable government. In 1716, George was at last able to visit Hanover again. The provision of the Act of Settlement that he could not leave Britain without the previous consent of Parliament had been abrogated rather shamefacedly by a unanimous vote. On his journey the King was accompanied by Stanhope and Bernstorff, Sunderland later finding a pretext to join them. Townshend and the other ministers remained in London, as did Bothmer, who was entrusted with writing confidential reports on the doings of the government. The British public were told then and on later occasions that the chief purpose of this journey was to enable the King to conduct foreign policy from a position nearer the centre of affairs, but nobody was deceived, and after a while the pretence was abandoned. Everyone knew that George felt more at home in Hanover than in England.

Back in his old capital, and in far more congenial surroundings, George tended even more to see things from a Hanoverian viewpoint than an English one. Stanhope and Sunderland, thoroughly English though they were, had been removed from immediate contact with public opinion at home, and sometimes were inclined to follow their master's views and forget the severe restrictions under which politicians in London had to work. Bernstorff, of course, never saw Britain as anything else than a tool to further Hanoverian ambitions. A dichotomy developed between the ministers in London and Hanover.

Townshend was deeply troubled. In August, a pamphlet entitled *Remarks of an English Merchant* had appeared in which the King was accused of having used the British fleet in the Baltic to further Hanoverian ambitions. It was evident, according to the pamphlet, that so many ships had not been sent for the protection of commerce alone. The real reason was to bring Britain into foreign quarrels in order to extend the King's states in Germany, in spite of the fact that this might entail the destruction of a champion of the Protestant cause. Naval supplies could have been obtained from Archangel. Eight ships had been left behind in the Baltic when there were no British merchantmen left there to protect, and put under Danish command.[2] Nobody doubted that the material for this publication had been furnished by Gyllenborg, the Swedish ambassador. Apart from the fact that Archangel could hardly have been able to provide all the supplies needed at short notice, the pamphlet came too close to the truth for comfort. Townshend was the Secretary responsible for Northern affairs, and had signed the letter ordering Norris to detach the eight ships to join the Danish fleet. If Parliament were to enquire into the matter, not only might the government be overthrown, but an act of attainder might cost him his head. Matters were made worse by the publication of the Danish manifesto of 10 October 1716 which revealed that Norris had pressed the Tsar to invade Sweden. The British public were greatly perturbed and everyone expected that the government would come under severe attack during the coming session of parliament.[3] Townshend further feared that the public might hear that Polwarth, the new British ambassador to Denmark, had told the Danish king that in his opinion Britain would aid the Danes in the coming year in the same way as she had done in 1716.[4] This would have exasperated the people even more, but luckily the secret was kept.

The pressure on Townshend was so strong that he

thought of giving up office. He wrote to Stanhope that he wished to retire into the country, that the miserable and distracted condition into which the northern affairs were plunged gave the discontented hopes of raising some disturbance in Parliament, and that His Majesty was in danger of ruining his credit and influence: 'God knows we had no share in this northern quarrel.'[5] In a postscript to his letter, he complained of the difficulties created every day by their enemies about the King's person (i.e. the Hanoverians) and accused Bothmer of always having some infamous project afoot to get money.

The King was dissatisfied with Townshend, partly because he considered the minister's suggestion that he raise more troops in Hanover and come to an arrangement with the Tsar an impertinent interference in his German affairs (see Chapter 3). He also blamed him for delays in the conclusion of the treaty with France, though this may not have been Townshend's fault,[6] and perhaps because of his frequent mention of the Prince of Wales in his dispatches. Stanhope and Sunderland saw their chance. Only a few weeks earlier. Stanhope had been so despondent that he too, had decided to leave the government as soon as the King had returned to England.[7] Now he and Sunderland, both not fully apprised of the situation at home, thought they could do better than Townshend. They seem to have persuaded the King that they could conduct his German business according to his wishes. Even before the King had left Hanover, Townshend was informed that he had been appointed Lord Lieutenant of Ireland. This was a higher-ranking, but less influential post than Secretary of State. Stanhope tried to disguise the change as a promotion, but Townshend was not deceived, although he accepted for the time being.

Parliament had been prorogued several times, but when the King returned to London, no further delays were possible. The ministry had to look for a way to divert the coming storm over the management of the fleet in the Baltic, and even to persuade Parliament to grant money for another expedition in 1717. The only expedient they could think of was the arrest of the Swedish ambassador and the seizure of his papers. The ministers knew that Gyllenborg was in correspondence with the Jacobites. His mail had been opened, a common, if not exactly approved practice during the eighteenth century, and Townshend had sent copies of some letters to Stanhope.[8] The papers provided proof that the King of Sweden had been negotiating with the Pretender. Both were enemies of George I. The Jacobites lacked troops, while the King of Sweden was short of money. It was natural that they should try to supply each other's needs. Negotiations had been going on for some time and were to continue until Charles XII died. They never had a positive result because the Jacobites did not have sufficient money, and the Swedes could spare no troops. Nevertheless, the Gyllenborg letters, which were soon published, showed that an invasion of Scotland by Swedish troops had been under consideration. With anti-Jacobite feelings in the country still running high, this was enough to distract Parliament's attention, and provision for another Baltic expedition was granted, though only by a narrow majority of 153 to 149.

This was not quite the end of the affair. In 1722, during a debate in the House of Lords, a number of peers demanded that copies of the instructions given to the British fleet in the Baltic be put before the House. The ministry resisted the proposal strongly. An enquiry into the use of the navy during the Northern War would provide ammunition for the opponents of the dynasty, and might even endanger the lives of the ministers themselves. But they were pressed so hard that the only way out they could find was the assertion that the proposed procedure was improper, as it amounted to an enquiry whether the King had broken his coronation oath. This argument convinced most of the peers and the proposal was voted down. If Parliament were publicly to declare to the British people that their king had violated his solemn pledge to Britain in order to favour his home country, civil war would have been inevitable. Nevertheless, over twenty peers entered a formal protest, alleging the ancient principle that the Crown was inviolate, and only ministers could be held responsible. Needless to say, this argument did not cause the government to change its attitude.

During the debate on the naval supplies for 1717,

Townshend had remained silent, though voting with the government. On the next day, he received a letter from Stanhope announcing his dismissal. To the King's surprise, Walpole and several other ministers decided to leave the government together with Townshend. The Hanoverians, whom George had previously consulted, were equally astonished. They had not expected that so many men would resign from well-paid posts on a matter of principle.[9] Though not expressly stated as the reason for the mass resignation, this principle was resentment at Hanoverian interference in British affairs. This was made clear a few days later by Pulteney, one of the ministers who had resigned, when he declared in Parliament that he had hitherto remained silent as a servant of His Majesty, but that now he hoped that 'the resolution of a British Parliament would make a German ministry tremble'.

Stanhope and Sunderland managed to find enough support in Parliament to form a government, while the ministers who had resigned, in true eighteenth-century fashion, tried to make nuisances of themselves as much as possible in order to force their way back into office. For the time being, the Germans retained their place in the King's councils as they had in the past. Their position is illustrated by an anecdote we owe to Pendtenrieter, the Austrian ambassador: after the death of Charles XII, the Danes sent their minister von Holst to London to ask for financial aid to pursue the war against Sweden. He first applied to Bernstorff and Bothmer, who were inclined to favour the request, but as only Parliament could grant the money, the British ministers had to be consulted. A conference was held in which Bernstorff, Bothmer, Stanhope, and General Cadogan took part. The English were in a quandary. They said they would like to provide the money and aid the Electorate in order to remain in the King's favour, but they were responsible to Parliament, which might one day accuse them of treason if they went too far. The Germans insisted that the possession of the English throne brought their sovereign more grief than pleasure if no advantage were to accrue to the Electoral House after he had had to leave his own country and deprive his subjects of the consolation of his presence. The English answered apologetically that the nation had spent many millions in fitting out a squadron for the Baltic, in subsidies to the belligerents, and through loss of commerce. They were ready to go on doing what was agreeable to the King, but they should be allowed to save their face and not be forced to infringe the Act of Settlement. Otherwise the people would be antagonized and everything brought to ruin. They finally agreed to Holst's proposals, but with so many provisos that Pendtenrieter confidently predicted that nothing would ever come of these plans.[10] As related in the previous chapter, nothing ever did. Britain renewed its friendship with Sweden and the Danes had to make what peace they could.

On this occasion, the British gave an evasive answer to the Germans' wishes, but they were soon to take a firmer stand. Stanhope, who held the leading role in the government, was too great a statesman, too ambitious, and too good an English patriot to suffer his country to remain under foreign influence for long. Difficulties began in relation to the British embassy in Vienna. The ambassador, St. Saphorin, had already been informed that in future he should address his reports to the Secretaries of State instead of to Robethon (i.e. Bernstorff).[11] Relations between the British and the Hanoverian ministers became very strained when St. Saphorin, under orders from George I,[12] arranged an alliance between Hanover, Saxony-Poland, and Austria, ostensibly for mutual defence, but in reality directed against Russia and Prussia. The British ministers were indignant because they had not been informed about these negotiations, and especially angry, firstly because the British ambassador had been used for Hanoverian purposes and secondly because the treaty contained a clause making ratification by Saxony dependent on a formal British promise to defend Danzig and Elbing against the Russian fleet. In spite of desperate efforts by the Hanoverians[13] no British minister would sign such a promise, though the treaty seems to have been ratified even without it.

The final break with the Hanoverians came over relations with Prussia. When the King, on Stanhope's advice, was endeavouring to conclude a treaty with Prussia in order to obtain an ally against the Tsar, this policy was fiercely opposed by Bernstorff, who feared that a strong Prussia would be a danger to Hanover. The King took Stanhope's side. By now he felt secure on his royal throne, had learnt to see politics in a wider context than that of his Electorate, and had become aware of his responsibilities to his new and much more powerful country. He forbade his Hanoverians to interfere in any way with British politics. On 24 November 1719, the Duke of Newcastle could write: the King 'has told M. Bernstorff and the rest of the Germans that if ever they pretend in any manner whatsoever to meddle in English affairs, he will turn them out of his service ... the Germans have no more interest with him than the subjects of any other nation.'[14]

This should have been sufficient, but Bernstorff was not a man to give up easily. He thought of a plan to unseat the present ministry and to replace it with one more to his liking. The government he had in mind was to have two new Secretaries of State, while Townshend and Walpole were to be included in minor posts. Stanhope was to be reduced to Lord Privy Seal or a general of horse. Bernstorff wrote a letter to the Imperial Chancellor Count Sinzendorff with these proposals, asking for the help of Imperial troops from the Netherlands 'on any emergent occasion'. Several copies of this letter, differing slightly from each other, have been preserved,[15] but the original has never been found. It has therefore, been surmised that it was a fake, probably inspired by Townshend and Walpole in order to force their way back into the government. The truth may never be known, but it is not out of character for Bernstorff, who had once proposed making a prisoner of the Tsar, to have thought of such a scheme.

Stanhope and Sunderland had their doubts, for they 'upbraided' Townshend and Walpole with the matter, but the latter of course denied all knowledge.[16] In any case, the letter worried the ministers sufficiently to make them think of broadening their political base. Townshend and Walpole agreed to rejoin the government provided the King and the Prince of Wales, who had been quarrelling, made up their differences. George and his son were bullied into a public reconciliation,[17] and all was well. There was no longer an effective opposition, and the ministry could feel safe. The Hanoverians, who may have had their own plans for reuniting father and son, were not consulted and only informed about the changes when everything had been arranged.[18] Bernstorff tried to maintain a brave face, but was so discomfitted at the King's taking such an important step without his advice, that he did not return to England after George's next journey to Hanover.

When Stanhope died in 1721, and Sunderland the year after, Townshend and Walpole, both decidedly anti-Hanoverian, reigned supreme. Never again was a Hanoverian minister admitted to British councils as a matter of right. But the Kings of Britain remained Electors of Hanover, and the link between the two countries was maintained. The necessity to protect the dynasty's prestige as German princes was to influence British policy for another hundred years. Foreign affairs were once again directed by Townshend as Secretary for the North, while Walpole was First Lord of the Treasury, gradually acquiring the power of a modern prime minister. In time, he would push Townshend aside, but the next crisis in European politics was still chiefly handled by Townshend.

In April 1725, Spain and Austria, hitherto bitter enemies, concluded the Alliance of Vienna. The initiative for the alliance had come from Spain, who was dissatisfied with her position after the War of the Spanish Succession. She wanted to regain Gibraltar and Minorca, which she had been forced to cede to Britain, and had ambitions on her former territories in Italy. She also had a dynastic quarrel with France. In return for Austrian military assistance, Spain was prepared to supply Austria with money, give extensive commercial rights in her overseas dominions to a trading company recently founded at Ostend, and recognize the Pragmatic Sanction, by which the Emperor had settled the succession to all the Habsburg dominions on his eldest daughter, Maria Theresa. Maria Theresa was also to be betrothed to one of the King of Spain's younger sons. The reasons why Austria agreed to this treaty are more difficult to determine, and indeed it was strongly opposed by some of the Austrian ministers. Presumably Austria felt somewhat isolated and wanted to use this opportunity to confront her ancient enemy France on more equal terms.

The treaty of Vienna severely disturbed the peace of

Europe. The young King of France and the heir to the throne of Spain were both in poor health. If they were to die, the King of Spain's second son, Don Carlos, might become ruler of Spain, France and Austria. A block of states would be formed stronger than anything Europe had ever seen, all smaller countries would be in danger, and the Protestant religion might be suppressed. British opinion was further antagonized by the rights granted to the Ostend company, which went far beyond anything British merchants had ever obtained. It was feared they might be excluded from the Spanish colonies altogether.

Townshend lost no time in preparing countermeasures. By September of the same year, he had formed the Alliance of Hanover, in which Britain, France and Prussia agreed to oppose the Austro-Spanish ambitions. This again led to the second Treaty of Vienna in November, in which Austria and Spain pledged themselves to full cooperation in all foreign affairs. Each side was to consider the other's cause as its own. The treaty, which was to be kept secret, but did not remain so for long, also stipulated that because of the danger of hostilities, both countries were to be put on a war footing, with Spain to provide the necessary funds for the Emperor.

Things did not go well for the allies of Vienna. Austria did indeed succeed in detaching Prussia from the Alliance of Hanover after only a year, but Britain countered by bringing in Denmark and Sweden instead. The money promised by Spain for the pay of the Austrian troops did not arrive in time, as the British navy managed to delay the departure of the Spanish silver fleet from the West Indies by more than half a year. In spite of this commitment, British sea power was strong enough to make it possible to send a squadron of twenty-four ships of the line to the Baltic in order to prevent the Tsarina, Catherine I, from intervening in favour of the Emperor. She might have threatened Denmark, which Hanover was obliged to defend, and therefore Hanover itself. The British squadron blocked the port of Reval for months, while both sides maintained outwardly friendly relations. Russia had been kept out of the conflict. The Prussian King, now a friend of Austria, declared that if Britain sent a squadron to the Baltic in the following year

(1727), he would regard this as an insult and revenge himself on His Majesty's German dominions[19], but his Austrian friends did not encourage him. The French threatened to invade the Hohenzollern provinces on the Rhine, and Prussia remained quiet.

While Spain was eager to fight, nobody in Austria really wanted war. The Spanish payments, when they at last arrived, proved to be insufficient, moreover the Emperor could not bring himself to announce the engagement of his daughter to Don Carlos. Apart from her personal predilection for the Duke of Lorraine, who had grown up at the court of Vienna, the proposed marriage was strongly opposed by the Princes of the Empire, who feared a return of the bad old days under Charles V, when they had hardly been able to maintain their independence against the combined might of Austria and Spain. When it became clear that the planned marriage would not take place, Spanish payments ceased, and Spain made an alliance with France. The Emperor, left without an ally, signed the preliminaries of Paris in May 1727, and promised to suspend the operations of the Ostend company for seven years. The crisis seemed to be over, but tension was to continue for a few more years.

Hanover had been at variance with the Emperor even before the conclusion of the treaty of Vienna, because of an alleged infringement of Protestant rights in the Palatinate. When war was threatening between the allies of Hanover and Vienna, it was feared that the Electorate might be attacked. Parliament was told that Hanover was in danger of invasion because of a British quarrel and asked to provide aid for her defence. The opposition invoked the Act of Settlement, and Shippen tried to make the point that England was threatened by a monarch whose vassal was England's king. But Pelham, the future prime minister, told the House that the Act of Settlement did not imply that Hanover was to be deprived of British assistance for ever. In February 1726, both Houses passed a resolution assuring the King that if any part of his dominions, though not belonging to the Crown of Great Britain, should be attacked because their ruler was also King of England, they would stand by him and defend such territories. For the first time, the principle had been established that Britain must protect Hanover when that country was under menace because of its connection with Britain.

George I died in the spring of 1727, on the way to his beloved Hanover, where he was buried. He had been King for nearly thirteen years, and had had a successful reign. He had defended himself effectively against both domestic and foreign enemies, and firmly established himself on a throne which his descendants still occupy. Though he had not been able to win the hearts of his new subjects, his rule had been just and merciful. Under him Britain had become recognized as a stable and dependable country whose friendship was worth cultivating.

5

RELATIONS BETWEEN BRITAIN AND HANOVER — ATTEMPTS AT SEPARATION

By the time of George I's death, the relationship between Britain and Hanover had become established in a pattern that was to last for another hundred years. Both states remained completely separate, the only link between them being their common monarch. There was not even a treaty between the two countries before 1814.[1] Hanover did indeed demonstrate its connection with Britain by always using the royal titles together with the Electoral ones, and adopting the British flag with a Hanoverian emblem in the centre, but Britain did not reciprocate. There, the Electoral titles could only be used in treaties with foreign powers, and this was done even when Hanover was not directly concerned,[2] though the practice seems to have been dropped after some years. Nevertheless, the Personal Union formed a strong bond between the two states. It was impossible for them to go to war with each other or for one of them to form an alliance with an enemy of the other. Britain could not let her king's home territories be occupied by hostile forces and perforce had to defend the Electorate. This was of course known to her enemies and might incite them to attack Hanover. The two countries were thus willy-nilly forced into an alliance in which Britain, as the stronger partner, also became the dominant one.

The advantages and disadvantages of this arrangement were debated in Britain throughout the eighteenth century and beyond with much the same arguments. Opponents of the Personal Union claimed that it was an unnecessary burden which obliged Britain to take part in Continental affairs of no interest to her, that Electoral business prevented the king from devoting his whole attention to his kingdom, and that the money and the troops employed to protect Hanover might have been used more profitably elsewhere. The acquisition of Bremen and Verden with the help of the British fleet was considered a particularly glaring example of this misdirection of British resources. On the other hand, those in favour of the Union pointed out that Britain must in any case have allies on the Continent in order to maintain herself against France. If France should ever succeed in dominating Europe, the ruin of British trade must follow. It was to Britain's advantage to have at her disposal a body of troops whose loyalty could always be relied upon. Bremen and Verden were valuable acquisitions, so valuable that Cromwell had once thought of occupying them for Britain. With the two duchies in friendly hands, the mouths of the Elbe and Weser rivers could never be closed to British shipping. In the possession of the Electorate, Bremen and Verden would further help to protect Hamburg from Danish ambitions, while at the same time it was important to prevent another power, especially Prussia, from occupying Denmark's entire frontier with the continent and thus gaining an undue influence over the country which controlled the Sound. These arguments seemed to have persuaded British statesmen, for none of them ever made a serious effort to break up the Personal Union.

When in opposition, politicians would indeed often inveigh against the Hanover connection, declaring that the Electorate had a pernicious influence on British policies, that it was insufferable for a great kingdom to be dependent on a small principality, that the Hanoverians were a beggarly people only interested in wringing as much money out of Britain as they could, and that Hanoverian troops might one day be used to suppress British liberties. Even if these arguments were meant seriously at the time they were uttered, they were forgotten as soon as the same politicians entered the government. The charges can therefore be dismissed as no more than a convenient weapon against which ministers found it difficult to defend themselves. Perhaps modern politicians must cultivate a reputation for consistency, but it was not always so in the eighteenth century.

The people of Britain were not interested in Hanover. They might grumble when the King remained absent for too long a time, but their discontent was forgotten as soon as His Majesty returned to London. The pages of the *Gentlemen's Magazine* and the *Annual Register*, publications widely read at the time, provide proof of this indifference, for they contain a considerable amount of information about the most diverse topics, such as the Indians of Patagonia, but practically nothing about Britons' fellow subjects in Hanover. In 1719, a committee headed by the Lord Chancellor came to the conclusion that it was doubtful whether the people of Great Britain could be persuaded that the Union would be prejudicial to the kingdom, 'but it seemed most probable that they would be pretty indifferent about the separation.'[3] If this was the people's attitude only a few years after the Union had been formed, it seems safe to assume that it remained the same until it was dissolved. The English certainly disliked all foreigners, and were easily aroused against them, but Hanoverians, unlike the ubiquitous Scots, were too rarely met with to keep any popular antagonism alive for long.

Even in the absence of formal ties, Britain and Hanover tended to cooperate, as was only natural under the conditions in which they found themselves. British and Hanoverian diplomats generally worked together, exchanging information, pursuing the same policies, and sometimes substituting for each other, often receiving special instructions to act in concert.[4] British consuls would also look after Hanoverian interests and were officially empowered to do so in the nineteenth century.[5] Outside the diplomatic field, cooperation tended to be more sporadic and depended on circumstances. An interesting example is the role of the post office at Nienburg, a small town on the river Weser. Nienburg lay on the postal route from Paris to Stockholm, on which couriers were seldom used because of the expense. The local postmaster had become adept at opening letters and forging the seals required for closing them again. The information he obtained from the diplomatic correspondence was very valuable to both Hanover and Britain, especially during the Seven Years' War, when France and Sweden were allied against Britain and Prussia. Furthermore, Nienburg often supplied faked seals for the use of postal authorities in Britain.[6] During the second half of the century, this collaboration gradually diminished and finally ceased, fakers in London having improved their skill.

Bothmer had lingered on as Hanoverian ambassador to Britain until 1732, but with little or no influence, and no successor was appointed. Liaison between Hanover and the King was the task of the German Chancery, instituted early in the reign of George I. The head of the Chancery, always of ministerial rank, was regarded as a personal servant of the king, and his office was located at the palace of St. James until it was removed to Buckingham Palace with the court. The minister was assisted by a Chief Secretary, an Under Secretary, both men with a university education, and several German underlings, the only English person in the office being the 'necessary woman' who did the cleaning. A plan preserved at Hanover[7] shows that the minister worked in a room 19 feet by 14 feet in size, preceded by a small ante-room which served as a waiting room and also contained filing cabinets. The Chief Secretary had a slightly larger room with more filing cabinets. Lower ranks seem to have occupied space on another floor. All members of the Chancery were paid out of the king's privy purse, i.e. from English funds. This was not quite in accordance with the Act of Settlement, but nobody seems to have minded. All in all, the German Chancery received between £100 and £120 a week. The greater part of the money went to the minister himself, whose pay amounted to £200 per twenty-eight-day month, with decreasing amounts for the lesser grades, those at the bottom of the scale being paid £19 per twenty-eight-day month, and one, a menial responsible for the supply of coal and candles, only half of this. One ex-employee enjoyed a quarterly allowance of £12 10s. The Privy Purse also paid for the Hanoverians' stationery, their coal, their candles, and their inland postal charges. These figures are from the royal archives at Windsor, which I was able to consult by gracious permission of Her Majesty. They refer to the year 1767, but there can be little doubt that similar conditions obtained throughout the Personal Union.[8]

Hanoverians had greeted the news that their Elector had become king of a powerful country with joy. They felt that their state had grown considerably in importance and now had a voice in the councils of Europe. The ministers proudly assumed the title of *Königlich Grossbritannische Churfürstliche Braunschweig-Lüneburgsche Geheime Räthe*, and considered themselves superior to their neighbours who could sport no such titles. As the years passed, however, people gradually came to realize that the Electorate had no influence on British policies, while its own foreign policy was subordinate to the wishes of Britain. Though Hanover was never treated as a colony, no Britons except the occasional volunteer army officer were ever appointed to posts in the Hanoverian service, and its internal administration was left undisturbed, the Electorate had become a satellite country.

This state of affairs made little difference to the common people, who did not expect to be consulted in political matters and simply remained loyal to their monarch, even when — after 1755 — they did not see him for more than seventy years. The attitude of the nobility, who alone had access to higher posts in the civil and military service, was somewhat different. They were aware that the rise of the Elector to royal rank had entailed a loss of importance for his lands in Germany, and a feeling of resignation among officials was not uncommon. Corruption and inactivity were widespread. Administrative business was slowed down because all matters of any importance had to be referred to London. Under normal conditions, it took about three weeks before an answer to a letter from the town of Hanover arrived, and the post was often delayed. If a problem arose elsewhere in the Electorate, months might elapse before an answer reached the local authorities.

On his departure George I had left behind a *réglement* according to which the Electorate was to be governed. Day-to-day administration was left to the council of ministers, but all important matters were to be referred to the King in London. According to the *réglement*, these included appointments in the army and the civil service, recommendations for pardon in cases of sentences to death, mutilation or torture, financial matters, and much else that today would be considered of minor consequence. Ministers solved the problem of distinguishing between important and unimportant matters by submitting practically everything to the king's decision, including such trivial cases as the desertion of a cornet of horse or the right to brew beer for the preachers of Hanover city. One would like to know how the tiny Chancery managed to cope with the flood of information that arrived from Hanover, but no such information seems to have come down to us.

In actual practice, the ministers were left pretty much to themselves, at least when the King was in London. There he had to depend on his ministers' reports for information. It was not difficult to write these in such a manner that the King was likely to agree to the proposals for further action which always accompanied the reports, and in fact he nearly always did so. When the King sent commands that were not replies to reports from Hanover, they obviously had to be interpreted, and his ministers and the King often misunderstood each other. They lived in different political climates. Hanoverians, used only to the conditions within the Empire, could not understand the wider view of world affairs that the King as head of a great power must acquire. They failed to grasp the intricacies of English politics. When George II, in 1746, was obliged to reinstate the Pelham ministry, which he had practically forced to resign two days earlier, the Hanoverian minister von Lenthe wrote to a friend that such things had never happened before, there was no example in history. 'This can lead to no good, and I cannot sufficiently commiserate with our dearest King.'[9] When ministers found orders from the king unpalatable, they still had to obey them without question, but not necessarily with alacrity. With the long delay in communication and the obsequious tone of the dispatches, the execution of the king's wishes could consciously or unconsciously be protracted for many months before the king discovered that the ministry had not followed his instructions, and by then the matter might be forgotten. Under such circumstances, the Hanover government gradually became more and more independent, at least with regard to internal affairs, and the saying arose that 'orders which cross the sea lose their force'.

Ministers at Hanover were appointed for life. Though each minister exercised authority over a particular department, all important decisions were made jointly. There was thus no personal responsibility and no incentive to hard work. Ministers were well paid and could lead a comfortable existence, many of them reaching the age of eighty, which was very high for the times. They generally met in the morning to discuss matters on hand, leaving the drafting of documents to their secretaries in the afternoon. While there were several ministers who were devoted to their work, this system was not likely to ensure efficient administration. It was said that in Hanover it was difficult to obtain a high position in the service of the government, but impossible to lose one. In effect, the Electorate was ruled by a clique of nobles, a type of government which has always tended to be very conservative. Many ambitious young men found such conditions too stultifying, and left Hanover to take service elsewhere. The most famous of these was von Hardenberg, who went on to become Chancellor of Prussia. He resigned from the Hanoverian service claiming that he could not make himself useful there in a manner that would satisfy him. In fairness to Hanover, it must be added that some extramarital adventures in London had endangered his prospects in the Electoral service. The Prussian minister von Stein's gibe that Hanover was the China of Europe was not, however, justified, as conditions in other minor German states were much the same.

It was only very rarely that one of the Hanoverian ministers travelled to London for consultation, and this soon led to the impression that they were not at the centre of affairs. The feeling of inferiority towards powerful Britain was reinforced by occasional lapses on the part of the King or his British ministers. Thus George II guaranteed the peace of Dresden with Prussia in 1745 both as King and Elector without consulting his Hanoverian ministers. In 1742, Hanoverian soldiers were taken into British pay without consulting the Electoral ministry, and three months later, the ministers had not even been informed of the conditions under which their troops were serving.[10] On both occasions, ministers felt slighted, and similar occurrences were not rare.

As a poor country subordinate to a much richer one, the Electorate was not above making an occasional profit from the connection, an attitude encouraged especially under George II, who upheld the principle that his German purse must never lose or be hazarded. Of the subsidies paid by Britain for the services of the Hanoverian troops, a part usually ended up in the coffers of the Electoral treasury. During the War of the Austrian Succession, when Britain had granted £310000 for the Electoral troops in the Netherlands, von Lenthe complained that only 150000 Thalers of this would be left for Hanover, 'this seems to me only a small profit'.[11] In fact, the Electoral war chest was enriched by a net profit of nearly one million Thalers (approximately £210000) during the years from 1742 to 1745.[12] Nevertheless, English accusations that Hanover was only interested in receiving subsidies were scarcely justified. Other German states from whom Britain hired troops also tried to profit from these contracts, apart from the special subsidies they were granted, but Hanover did not receive. It seems to have been a regular practice to station an army officer at the capital of such states in order to ensure that the money was properly spent.[13]

It is generally asserted that the Electoral minister resident in London was able to exercise an undue influence on the king because of his proximity to the royal person. There appears to be no evidence for this before the era of Count Münster in the nineteenth century. The London representative was always chosen from among the ministers themselves, and rejoined the ministry on his return. While the man in London had to be of exceptional stature to be agreeable to the King, the Chief Ministers were always careful to select someone who could not challenge their own position when he returned, von Munchhausen appointing his brother. We may even suspect that the London Chancery was intentionally restricted in personnel and overloaded with work in order to prevent it from developing ideas of its own. The

London minister was not permitted to sign letters to Hanover, he could only countersign orders issuing from the King, though he might occasionally add an explanatory note.[14]

Though Hanover was not always happy about its subordinate role in the Union, no one there ever suggested abolishing it. After all, Britain also protected the Electorate and enabled the nobles, who alone had any say in political matters, to enjoy their estates in peace. Initiatives for a separation of the two crowns came from the monarchs themselves.

George I had only been on the British throne for a year and a half when he took a first step towards the dissolution of the Union by making a will, dated 14/25 January 1716. He began by explaining why he was deviating from his father's last dispositions, which had prescribed primogeniture. Circumstances had changed as his father could not have known that his son would become King of Great Britain. The will goes on to say that it was easily to be foreseen, and had already been partly proved by events, that in the future George's German lands would fall into decline and that in time they would become a subject province of Britain. His dear and loyal German subjects would not fare well without a head of state of their own. After expressly stating that he had but one son, who also had only one son, George stipulated that if ever one of his descendants should leave two sons, the elder was to inherit the kingdom, while the second was to become Elector. Until this happened, a court under a Regent belonging to the Guelf family was always to be maintained at Hanover in order to retain money in the country and keep it in circulation, and also to provide a place where talented men could be trained in the service of the state.

George must have had some doubts about the validity of his testament, for only a few weeks after he signed it, he ordered his Hanoverian envoy to Vienna to consult the president of the Aulic Council about it. Unfortunately not all of this correspondence has survived,[15] but we know that both the president and the Emperor considered it impossible to force the first-born to give up the succession to the Electorate. Such a course would contravene the *Aurea Bulla*. But if the King could come to an arrangement with the British nation about the succession in the way he wished, this would be agreeable to the Emperor.

George ordered his envoy to represent to the president that as for the time being the British nation did not wish for a separation of the two crowns, the only means of effecting this was a testament. With regard to the *Aurea Bulla*, its intention was to prevent a division of the Electoral territories, and the installation of a junior line in Hanover would in no way contravene this principle. Kingdoms and principalities were of a nature quite different from private inheritances. The guiding rule must be that the prince was there for the people. The order of succession ought therefore to be in accordance with the welfare of the people and the countries to be governed, something which would not be the case if one country were to be perpetually annexed to another distant one. These thoughts, which show George I to have been a wise, benevolent and conscientious monarch — even if the letter was drafted by Bernstorff — were well received at the Imperial court, but no further action was taken. The Emperor consented to take a copy of the will into his custody, remarking that he could not act as executor, as he had no knowledge of its contents. George sent a copy of the testament to Vienna, where it was kept in the Imperial treasury.

Three years later George followed the suggestion of the Imperial court and asked his British ministers for an opinion on the validity of the will according to English law. After holding a conference, the Lord Chancellor wrote a report[16] which begins by sidestepping the question whether a separation would be expedient — this being a matter for the King's own judgement. After professing ignorance of the laws of the Empire, the report then states that the King's wish to abolish female succession in England could easily be complied with, but that it would be difficult to require a son who had succeeded his father as King to give up his rights to Hanover. If the abjuration of his rights to the

Electorate were to be made a condition of the king's heir occupying the British throne, this would lead to an inter-regnum, which was abhorrent to the British constitution, even if the interval was only a short one. If the successor were a minor incapable of taking an oath, the interregnum might last for years, with unforeseeable consequences. If the heir presumptive were required to take the oath during his father's lifetime, this could lead to quarrels among the royal family. A Prince of Wales unwilling to give up Hanover might look for ways and means to repeal the act of succession by which his abjuration would have to be prescribed. If would also be dangerous to try to convince Parliament that the Personal Union ought to be dissolved. Such an attempt could lead to a reaction, and Parliament might press for an immediate separation, causing immense difficulties.

The King was not entirely satisfied, and asked for the problem to be re-examined.[17] In their answer, the ministers started from the premise that no British law could alter the order of succession prescribed in the Empire. If the second son of a king were to inherit Hanover according to George's testament, but this was not in accordance with the laws of the Empire, he might have to be put on his Electoral throne by force. But Parliament would never sanction a war to put a prince in possession of territories that were not rightfully his. Furthermore, a king who according to German law was also Elector could easily obtain an Act of Parliament declaring his former resignation null and void. This again might entail the danger that such a king could try to convince Parliament that the retention of the German provinces was necessary for British trade. If this were to happen, Hanover would be degraded to a British province, and Parliament might legislate for it. The ministers were pleased to note that George declared himself satisfied with their report.

Two things may be deduced from the ministerial memorials: firstly, they were not particularly anxious to find a way to dissolve the Personal Union; and secondly, they did not want to annex the Electorate.

In the following year (1720), the King added a codicil to his will, reinforcing his provisions for a separation of the crowns by stipulating that if the Electoral line descended from a second son should die out, the succession was not to revert to the elder (i.e. British) line, but that the descendants of a third son should succeed. He added a number of complicated clauses regulating the position of the regent, who was to rule Hanover while the King and the Elector was the same person. These clauses seem intelligible only if it is assumed that George did not foresee that his second grandson, the future Duke of Cumberland, would be born during the following year, for they can be construed to mean that the Duke of Brunswick-Wolfenbuttel — head of the elder Guelf line — was entitled to rule the Electorate until the second grandson reached the age of twenty-five, i.e. for a possible twenty years. This part of the will may have caused difficulties for George II after his accession.

A copy of the codicil was sent to Vienna, while at the same time the Archbishop of Canterbury and the Duke of Brunswick each received a copy of the will and the codicil. The accompanying letter to Brunswick mentions that the testament contains dispositions affecting the entire Guelf family and therefore the Duke himself. He is asked to inform the Hanover ministry of his possession of the will after George's death and to have it opened by one of the ministers in his presence.[18] A letter to the King of Prussia[19] mentions that George had appointed him, together with the Emperor and the Duke of Brunswick, as executors, though this is not stated in the will.

George still had doubts about the validity of his testament, and on 27 December 1720 asked Bernstorff, who still retained his confidence, for his opinion. Bernstorff wrote two memoranda, which do not differ greatly from each other. He regarded the separation of the two crowns as feasible. According to him, the intention of the *Aurea Bulla* was merely to ensure the indivisibility of the Electoral territories and the undisputed right of succession; the possibility of an Elector becoming king of a foreign country and thereby losing his German nationality according to Natural Law was not foreseen. Such a monarch was therefore at liberty to alter the succession, provided the Electoral dominions remained unimpaired. It was, however, necessary to obtain the consent of the Emperor and come to an arrangement with the Estates of Hanover. Bernstorff considered a separation desirable, as no monarch could submit his country to foreign domination with a good conscience. He cited Ireland, Scotland and Portugal as instances of unhappiness under foreign rule. Bernstorff did not think much of the appointment of a regent, and even less of the nomination of foreign princes as executors. Such arrangements would only lead to quarrels and outside interference in the affairs of the House of Hanover.

The question of a dissolution of the Personal Union was not taken up again for another twenty years. Walpole's attempt to sound out Speaker Onslow in 1741 about Parliament's reaction to a proposal to separate the two crowns may be dismissed as a last-minute effort to save his ministry. Onslow's reply that this would 'seem like a message from Heaven' has often been quoted, but it seems to reflect his own opinion rather than the feelings of the public. But after the battle of Dettingen in 1743, the opposition, led by Pitt, raised such a violent storm against the Hanoverian connection that George II began to worry. He ordered his Hanoverian ministers to consider whether an Act of Parliament prohibiting the same person from succeeding to both the Kingdom and the Electorate would have legal force in the Empire.

The ministers began their answer[20] with a description of the disadvantages separation would entail for Britain, though admitting that such considerations were none of their business. British involvement in German troubles was unavoidable. Should France succeed in her aim of subjecting Germany, British commerce would be ruined. This danger was particularly great at the present time because the new Bavarian Emperor was allied with France. The weaker German states, especially the Protestant ones, which had hitherto looked to the Empire for protection must now depend upon Britain. Under such circumstances it was to Britain's advantage to have a reliable ally in Germany, especially as the weaker party, Hanover, must always defer to the wishes of the stronger, Britain. A few years earlier (i.e. in 1741), the Electorate might have derived great advantages from an alliance with Prussia, but these had had to be sacrificed to the political intentions of the King and the English nation. The ministers went on to assert that the legal situation was extremely difficult. While the heir to the kingdom might give up his rights to the Electorate if he wished to do so, he could not, according to the laws of the Empire, surrender the rights of his descendants, neither of those living, nor of those yet to be born.

The King acknowledged the receipt of his ministers' memorandum on 17 March 1744, but then let the matter rest. The storm against Hanover had died down. Pitt was soon to be given a minor office and held his peace. Nothing more was heard of plans to separate the two crowns until in September 1757[21] Philipp A. von Munchhausen, the Hanoverian minister in London, wrote to his brother, the Chief Minister, that the King had again asked for the ministry's views on a possible dissolution of the Personal Union. They were to answer two questions: first, whether a separation could be made legally effective, and second, whether a separation would be of advantage to the Electorate. This enquiry came at a time when Hanover had been occupied by French troops, and the King was negotiating for a separate peace with Austria, an action which would have aroused violent antagonism in England if it had become known there.

This time the ministers sent separate replies, probably because some of them had taken refuge in the fortress of Stade. With regard to the legal question, they all agreed that the heir to the British throne might renounce his claim to the Electorate, but only after he had come of age. He could not, however, waive the rights of a son already living, and it was doubtful if he could do so for a son yet unborn.

As to the advisibility of a separation for the Electorate, all the ministers concurred that Hanover had so far done well under the Personal Union, though opportunities for territorial acquisitions which had occurred had been missed because the English had been opposed to them. Some fear was expressed that when a king who had not been born in Hanover (i.e. the future George III) succeeded to the British throne, the Electorate might undergo the fate of Bremen and Verden, and, more recently, Hesse under Swedish rule, or Poland under Saxon rule. Those territories had seen their resources diverted to the more powerful country, and had suffered considerably. But the King of England was rich, and did not need the revenue from Hanover. In the past, significant sums had been saved because there was no court at Hanover, and it was to be hoped that this state of affairs would continue. A dissolution of the Union was only desirable if the present unnatural alliance between Austria and France were to endure after the war. If that were to come about, an Electorate tied to Great Britain would become a target for attack by Britain's enemies, safety could only be found in an alliance with Austria, and the link with Britain would have to be broken. But if the old system were eventually restored, with Britain and Austria once more allied against Britain's eternal enemy, France, the Electorate would fare better if the Personal Union remained intact.

From this it may be concluded that Hanoverians, or at least the Hanoverian nobility, were reasonably content with the British connection. One minister even expressed the hope that the King-Elector might one day introduce the English principle of the Rule of Law into the Electorate. By the time the ministers' opinions had reached London, the peace negotiations with Austria had failed, and Britain and Hanover were fighting the French as allies. The question of a dissolution of the Personal Union was dropped and never again officially discussed. Both George II and George III might on occasion declare they wanted to abdicate the throne in Britain and retire to Hanover, but these pronouncements were only the result of momentary frustration. Nobody ever took them seriously.

6

THE REIGN OF GEORGE II

George II was a dapper little man, thoroughly convinced of his political and strategic talents, but too weak or too wise to oppose effective resistance to the wishes of his British ministers. Personally brave, he envisioned a distinguished military future for himself. One of his great aims in life was to be as different from his father as he could, but like many another son with the same ambition, he became as like him as was humanly possible. Few modern English schoolchildren would be able to name any significant difference between the two monarchs.

The King liked to dabble in foreign affairs, once telling the Austrian ambassador that he knew much more about the situation on the Continent than his English ministers, and that the ambassador could always come directly to him when European politics were concerned.[1] George's claim to better knowledge was probably justified, for he received regular reports from his Hanoverian envoys, which he could, and generally did, keep secret from his British ministers. But we may doubt whether it was proper for a constitutional monarch to withhold pertinent information from his ministers, especially when such information might influence his decisions as head of the government. Constitutional propriety was certainly violated when the King received secret reports from a British diplomat on Anglo-Russian affairs. When ambassador to St Petersburg, Lord Hyndford regularly sent him news about the international situation, interlaced with the occasional spicy story about the Russian court. These letters were transmitted via Hanover in order to keep them from coming to the knowledge of the British ministers. George showed his gratitude by seeing to it that the impoverished lord's arrears of salary were promptly paid.[2] But all this was little more than playing at politics. In practice the control of British foreign policy was firmly in the hands of the cabinet.

In England the new reign had an auspicious start. The King was often to be seen riding abroad on his horse or in his carriage, and boating on the Thames. He spoke at length in Parliament. The people were delighted with this change from the late king's lifestyle. 'In seven years in this country, I have never seen such universal contentment', reported a member of the Austrian embassy.[3] But this happy state of affairs was not to last. In 1729, George made his first journey to the land of his birth, which he had not seen for fifteen years. When he came back, his attitude towards England had changed. 'Nothing English would please him', begins Lord Hervey's much quoted account of George's return from a later journey. He was dissatisfied with English gentlemen, English ladies, English horses, carriages, cooks, grooms, and much else. In short, he seems to have grumbled about everything except the English weather. All things were better in Hanover, where there were no regicides and republicans, and men did not have to be bribed to do their duty.

During his reign of thirty-three years, George made twelve journeys to Hanover, and would doubtless have travelled even oftener if he had not been prevented by war. He generally left in May or June, and returned in September or October. In Hanover, he would sometimes travel around the country, but more often he preferred the festivities and parades of Hanover city or went hunting from his castle in the Goehrde. The King's absences were accepted in England without too much opposition unless he stayed away too long, as he did in 1736 because he was suffering from the piles. People were especially upset because the King was not in England on his birthday, something that caused great distress to the shopkeepers and workmen who expected to make a major part of their profit on this occasion. There was considerable commotion among the public, and malcontents claimed that George despised the British nation. When the news came that the King's ship was in trouble because of a storm, there was more joy than sympathy on the faces of the people.[4] But as soon as the King was back, all discontent was forgotten.

One of the first acts of George II's reign was the suppression of his father's will. The story has often been told how the Archbishop of Canterbury presented his copy of it to the King in council, expecting it to be opened and read out. But the King merely put it into his pocket and walked out of the room with nobody daring to oppose him.

There was more trouble with the second copy, entrusted to the Duke of Wolfenbuttel. George must have feared some action on the part of the Duke, for within less than a month after his father's death, he had obtained a unanimous opinion of his Electoral ministers that the will was invalid. Under the King's orders the Duke of Newcastle, Secretary for the South, immediately wrote to H. Walpole, the ambassador to Paris, asking him to inform Cardinal Fleury, the French Chief Minister, of the Hanoverian opinion and enlist his aid against Wolfenbuttel, especially as the Duke might be assisted by the House of Austria (the Emperor was married to a Wolfenbuttel princess).[5] A few days later, the matter was made even more urgent when Walpole was asked to show the Cardinal an intercepted letter from the Duke of Wolfenbuttel to M. de Morville, the French foreign minister. The ambassador reported that Fleury showed his utmost 'detestation and astonishment' at those who had given his late Majesty such mischievous advice and assured Walpole of the French king's inviolable fidelity to His British Majesty, not forgetting to add that the people of Hanover might like the dispositions of the will. It appears safe to conclude that the Duke of Wolfenbuttel was acquainted with the contents of George I's testament, and was hoping to become Regent of Hanover, with French help, until the young Duke of Cumberland came of age.

Unfortunately both the Electoral ministers' memorandum and the letter to M. de Morville have disappeared. The Duke's copy of the letter was probably destroyed when the

Duchess, at his request, burnt some of his papers before his death.[6] It is, however, known that he asked the Hanover ministry to send a representative to open the will, and that they replied that at present the King was too busy to attend to minor matters. This remarkable statement has come down to us with a pencilled exclamation mark which may have been put there by the original reader.[7] Other documents at Wolfenbuttel show that the Duke was in close liaison with the Imperial court. They begin with the instructions to the chief minister, Count Dehn, who was to represent the Duke at the King's coronation. With regard to George I's will, Dehn was to say nothing, but merely to report what he heard. He was to offer no congratulations in the name of the Emperor (who had differences with Britain), as the Emperor was determined not to take the first step towards a reconciliation. A fortnight later, when Dehn had already left for England, he was sent a copy of a letter from the Imperial court, from which it appears that Vienna had asked the British government what it was to do with its copy of the testament, that it was thought there that his present Majesty was dissatisfied with his father's will, and that the Imperial government wanted to be informed about the attitude of the London court, though it was not prepared to make the slightest advances.[8]

Once assured of France's support, George was ready to come to an arrangement with Wolfenbuttel, and after protracted negotiations with Dehn, a lavish subsidy treaty was concluded with the Duke although at the same time the Duke was receiving subsidies from the Emperor, whose relations with Britain were little short of war. The King sent the completed treaty to Wolfenbuttel, but made it an absolute condition of ratification that his father's will must be sent to him unopened.[9] The will was promptly sent to England, and the treaty duly ratified. The whole affair was kept so secret that the Austrian Ambassador, who must have had excellent sources of information, reported that only ten men in the kingdom knew about it.[10]

Getting hold of the third copy, deposited with the Emperor at Vienna, was to take some time. Relations between Britain and the Empire were strained for some years after George I's death, and it seems that at first

George II did not make any attempt to gain possession of the testament. Only one reference to the matter has been found in the Vienna archives. It is a short note about a discussion in council on 15 August 1727[11] on what to do with the will. The council decided to inform Walpole and the King of Prussia, but we are not told whether the document was opened and read. When Anglo-Austrian friendship was about to be renewed in 1730, the Hanoverian ministers suggested that the King now ask for the will to be extradited. This time George was in no hurry. He ordered his Hanoverian envoy not to press the matter until certain problems pending between Hanover and the Empire had been settled. Once this had been done, the envoy was to declare that the will ought not to be published, as it contained stipulations not in accordance with the law, and that this had been mentioned by the Imperial court at the time of its deposition. If these stipulations became generally known, this might cause difficulties not for George II, but for his successors.[12] Apparently the document was handed over to the envoy according to the King's wishes, and forwarded to London. On 5 December 1737, all three copies of the will were sent to Hanover, where they are still preserved, but without the codicils.

Why was George so determined to keep his father's will secret? Once the danger of interference by the Duke of Wolfenbuttel had been removed, the testament contained nothing that affected him personally. There were plenty of precedents, including the will itself, to show that he could alter any provisions regarding his descendants which did not suit him. One possible explanation is that he wished to avoid a quarrel between his two sons, which might ensue if the Duke of Cumberland claimed his right to succeed to the Electorate. Although George hated his firstborn, Frederick Prince of Wales, and loved his second son, he seems to have been resolutely opposed to his succession in Hanover. Some proof of this is the fact that he disregarded a suggestion by the opposition in Parliament that he abandon his German territories and leave them to a younger son.[13] An article in the *Gentlemen's Magazine* for 1742 mentions His Majesty's dislike of surrendering Hanover to the Duke of Cumberland as the most obvious obstacle to such a project. It appears that the Duke was never shown his grandfather's will, for as late as 1760 he did not know where the copies had been deposited.[14] George did indeed twice make enquiries about a separation of the two crowns (see Chapter 5), but only when he was afraid of English antipathy to Hanover, and he dropped the matter as soon as conditions improved.

George's worries about the will may have been caused by something we do not know about. On 3 February 1728, the Austrian embassy reported that in his testament the late king had left a large sum of money to the Duchess of Kendal, that he had given orders that the Duke of Cumberland should leave for Hanover as soon as Prince Frederick, George II's elder son, arrived from there, and that he had charged the Duke of Wolfenbuttel to ensure that the administration of the Electorate should never fall into English hands. Furthermore, a petition was to be made to Parliament for the payment of his debts. Part of this story is certainly true, for George had made a private will (in 1723) in which he left £10000 in South Sea stock to the Duchess of Kendal (i.e. the Countess von Schulenburg), and an even larger sum to Sir Robert Walpole in trust for her.[15] If the rest of the embassy's account is also correct, the late king must have added another codicil to his public testament, which his son did not want published. Even if it is assumed that such a second codicil existed, this does not provide a satisfactory explanation for the suppression of the will. The Duke of Wolfenbuttel had been restrained, and George could easily countermand any instructions about his sons made by their grandfather. The embassy suggests that he feared trouble in Parliament, who would certainly enquire into the late king's personal fortune, which was known to be considerable, before paying his debts, but his successor had only the choice between paying these debts himself, or applying to Parliament, and Parliament would make enquiries whether it knew about the will or not.

The most probable solution to the problem is that George was worried about the rumour that his father had left a large amount of money to the Queen of Prussia, George II's sister.[16] Parsimonious by nature, he may have wanted to keep this money for himself, and at the same time prevent it from getting into the hands of Prussia, Hanover's most dangerous rival. He may have believed that this bequest was mentioned in the copies of the will and codicil or codicils deposited with the three trustees. When he found nothing in the first two copies, he would have lost interest, something which would explain his lack of eagerness to obtain the third copy. It is unlikely that such a bequest was actually made, for the Prussian king, and his son after him, made strenuous efforts to find evidence for it, but without success. Perhaps a document, such as a codicil to the private will, will one day be found to throw light on the matter.

☆　　　☆　　　☆

The diplomatic situation at the beginning of the new reign was still serious. Although the Emperor had signed the Preliminaries of Paris in May 1727, the ensuing Congress of Soissons, which was to settle all outstanding matters, showed that he was hoping for an understanding with France and a coalition of the Catholic powers against Britain and the Protestant states of Germany.[17] But Cardinal Fleury preferred to work for an alliance of the Bourbon kingdoms, France and Spain, while maintaining friendly relations with Britain. The congress dragged on for years because the Emperor, though his hopes of an alliance had faded, wanted at least to obtain the guarantee of his Pragmatic Sanction by the other states. Even when Britain, France, and Spain signed the Alliance of Seville in November 1729, and threatened war if the Emperor did not make concessions to Spain in Italy, he still held out. He only gave way when Britain concluded an alliance with him and at last agreed to recognize the Pragmatic Sanction. The treaty, signed at Vienna in 1731, guaranteed the Austrian possessions. It was disliked by France, who wished to isolate the Emperor, but for the time being, Anglo-French friendship continued outwardly undisturbed.

The Treaty of Vienna was the work of Walpole, who had managed to oust Townshend from the government. Walpole would in any case brook no rival, and there were differences between the two men. Townshend objected to friendship with the Emperor, while Walpole's chief preoccupation was maintaining peace. Walpole had public opinion on his side.

Parliament was becoming restive because of the high cost of keeping Britain on a war footing. Opposition speakers began to denounce the Electorate, holding forth wrongly, but effectively, on the name of the Treaty of Hanover that had been greeted with universal approval only a few years before. They claimed that the Act of Settlement was being infringed by paying Hessian troops enlisted only for the defence of the King's German dominions with British money. Townshend retired into private life, there to acquire another kind of fame as 'Turnip Townshend' for his successful efforts to spread the cultivation of that crop. The King was sorry to see him go because, unlike Walpole, he had supported his Continental policy. In a letter to Harrington, the new Secretary for the North, Newcastle wrote that the King had said that 'his dependence for Hanover must now be upon you and I'.[18]

While the congress of Soissons was still sitting, Britain and Prussia had nearly come to blows over Hanover. An originally insignificant dispute over grazing rights on some meadows near the Hanover-Prussian border was escalated when both sides took hostages. The Prussian king, Frederick William I, was a man of excitable and unpredictable character. The British ambassador to Berlin describes him as an arrogant, pompous bully, and only respect for royalty prevented him from calling the king a coward also. Frederick William was already incensed at George II because George had come to Hanover without informing Berlin of his arrival, something he claimed George I had always done, an assertion denied by Townshend, who had twice accompanied the late king. When Hanover took hostages, the Prussian King reacted violently and threatened to attack the Electorate. King George was equally hot-tempered and would not give way to a brother-in-law whom he disliked, not least because his sister was being badly treated at the Berlin court. However, the story that the two kings spoke of each other as 'my brother the corporal', and 'my brother the dancing-master', and were only with difficulty prevented from fighting a duel, is probably not true. George asked for British support and was promised the assistance of British-paid troops from Hesse and Denmark, as well as British forces.[19] The British ambassadors to Paris and Stockholm were asked to enlist the aid of the French and Swedish governments, who both agreed to put pressure on Prussia. Even the Dutch were willing to threaten Prussian Cleves. Frederick William, on the other hand, found no friends who would help him. His Saxon allies told him that he had brought the quarrel upon himself, while the Austrians were lukewarm. After six months of blustering, he had to come to a peaceable arrangement, but was allowed to save his face by being permitted to release his hostages twenty-four hours after his Prussians had been set free. For a time it had seemed as though Europe would be set in flames because of Hanover.

In the world of eighteenth-century politics, it is not surprising that this dispute only temporarily interrupted negotiations for a double marriage between the two Crown Princes of Britain and Prussia and the eldest daughters of the two kings. The idea had first been suggested by the Prussian king, who wanted his son (the future Frederick II) to marry a British princess. George was agreeable, but only if his son could also marry the Crown Prince's sister. Frederick William, however, would only consent to a double marriage if his son were made governor of Hanover. This demand was too much for George, but he proposed that he would appoint Frederick's bride, the Princess Royal, to govern the Electorate if the marriage could take place. Sir Charles Hotham was sent to Berlin to work out an arrangement, but Frederick was not destined to reside at Hanover. In a fit of pique at Hotham's interference in Prussian affairs, and because Hotham tried to ensure better treatment for the Queen, George's sister, Frederick William decided to call off all marriage plans. On receiving the news, the British court haughtily informed him[20] that a marriage would never have been considered if it had not been proposed by Prussia.[21]

Only two years after the alliance of Vienna had been concluded, Europe was at war, nominally over the succession of Louis XV's father-in-law to the throne of Poland. This war is called the War of the Polish Succession, but it had little to do with Poland, where France was powerless. It was rather a concerted attack on the Austrian dominions by France, Spain, and Sardinia (Savoy). The Emperor naturally asked for help from his new British ally, but in spite of the King's eagerness and an attempt at persuasion by Hattorf, Walpole refused to join the fighting. His refusal may have been justified because of the danger of another Jacobite rebellion aided by France, but it did not enhance Britain's reputation as a reliable ally. The official reason given for the failure to assist Austria was that Britain could not go to war without the Netherlands, and public opinion agreed with this.[22]

George II did, however, come to the Emperor's aid as Elector, and sent troops to the Rhine. But there was not much fighting, probably because the allies were afraid that the Russians might interfere on Austria's behalf. When peace was made, the Emperor had to cede Lorraine to France against a French guarantee of the Pragmatic Sanction, and exchange Naples and Sicily for Parma, Piacenza, and Tuscany. This transfer was not necessarily a loss for Austria as the provinces in Northern Italy were more easily defendable, but the net result of the war was a decrease of British influence on the Continent, and a weakening of Austria. The Turks saw their chance and shortly afterwards forced Austria to give back a large part of the territories, including the city of Belgrade, she had won from them twenty years before. This time the peace was mediated by France, while the earlier one had been arranged with British help.

A war far more dangerous to the stability of Europe was to follow some months after the succession of Frederick II to the throne of Prussia, in 1740. Frederick was young and ambitious. Three of his grandparents were Guelfs, but he was not interested in genealogy, he wanted fame and power, not caring how he could obtain them. He had inherited a territory of some 130000 square kilometres and 2.5 million inhabitants, together with a well-filled treasury and a standing army of 70000 men, superbly trained and equipped. He looked for a chance to employ these resources.

Immediately after Frederick's accession, von Munch-hausen, the Hanoverian Chief Minister, travelled to Berlin, following instructions he had received six years before. His mission was to congratulate the new king, to renew the *foedus perpetuum* of 1693 between Hanover and Brandenburg, and to sound out Frederick's intentions. He received only vague answers, Frederick preferring to send an emissary to Hanover, where George II had arrived for his summer visit.[23] The emissary asked for a guarantee of Frederick's succession to Julich-Berg, East-Frisia, and Mecklenburg, offering to assist George elsewhere in return. The Hano-verian ministers advised the King to give the required assurance for Julich-Berg, reasoning that an increase of Prussian power on the Rhine would be harmless for the Electorate, but useful for Germany as a bulwark against France. For East-Frisia, where George had claims of his own, they suggested a compromise, while Mecklenburg could be discussed in due course. As to what was to be asked from Prussia in return, the ministers made only a very guarded statement, but it seems clear that they hoped for territorial gains for Hanover, but did not dare to say so as the guarantee would have to be given by Great Britain.[24]

Negotiations were interrupted when George returned to London. Evidently the British cabinet favoured the propo-sals, for George wrote to the ministry asking whether Hanoverian interests could be protected if an Anglo-Prussian alliance were formed. They answered that the important thing was to gain Frederick's adherence to an anti-French league. Electoral interests could be attended to later on. A minister should be sent to Berlin to conclude a treaty.[25]

Nothing was to come of these plans, for in the meantime the opportunity Frederick had been waiting for had arrived. In October 1740, the Emperor Charles VI died at an unexpectedly early age, leaving the Empire without a head. His daughter Maria Theresa inherited all the Habsburg dominions, and hoped to have her husband, Francis of Lorraine, elected as Emperor. Her succession had been guaranteed by all the European powers except Bavaria, but it soon became apparent that these guarantees were not to be relied upon.

Frederick began preparations for war in November. When the British ambassador expressed his disquiet, he was told that Frederick did not feel bound by his father's engagements, and if the King of Britain disapproved of his views, he was ready to go to war with him, i.e. attack Hanover.[26] On 16 December 1740, Frederick marched his troops into the Austrian province of Silesia, proclaiming that he did so in order to maintain the peace and protect Maria Theresa's inheritance. The Austrians drily replied that if sending an army into one's neighbour's tranquil countryside was the way to maintain peace, they would like to know how to disturb it, and prepared to defend their territory. They did not know how many enemies they would have to face.

The Hanoverian ministers were aghast. They wrote to the King that they deplored his absence at such a critical juncture. Prussia was a danger to all her neighbours. They suggested mediation between Austria and Saxony in order to unite them against Prussia, and coordination of British and Hanoverian interests, while care should be taken that Prussia should not fall into French hands.[27] When George asked for a formal opinion, they wrote that the *casus foederis* according to the Pragmatic Sanction was undoubtedly given. The King's glory and his reputation for reliability were at stake. But they were careful to add that the King's guarantee had been given jointly with others, and that if he acted alone, his German dominions would be in great danger. They advised him to temporize until it became clear that the other guarantors of the Pragmatic Sanction were prepared to assist him. At the same time they suggested that this might be a favourable time to acquire the neighbouring ecclesiastical territory of Hildesheim.[28] Negotiations were set on foot between the Hanoverian minister in London and the Austrian ambassador there for Austrian aid in case the Electorate were invaded, and even for a joint attack on Prussia and a division of the spoils.[29]

While these negotiations were still going on, the Hanoverians began to have doubts. They wrote to the King that Prussia was assembling troops at cities near the frontier of the Electorate, while Vienna was without power, without money, without men, without generals, and worst of all, without good counsel. They advised gaining time by dissimulation.[30] When Frederick sent a special envoy to Hanover to renew the old treaties of friendship, the ministers at first suspected that he was only trying to deceive them in order to gain time. But when he assured them of his king's friendship, and asked for King George's good offices to persuade the Queen of Hungary (Maria Theresa) to cede Lower Silesia with the city of Breslau to Prussia, and further promised to maintain the House of Austria and elect her husband Francis as Emperor, they wrote to the King that an alliance with Prussia would be the lesser evil.[31] But all Hanoverian hopes for a peaceful accommodation and perhaps an increase of territory were dashed when in April the King wrote to his ministers that Parliament was about to decide on measures highly offensive to Prussia, and that they must prepare for military action.[32]

In Britain, the news of Frederick's march into Silesia had aroused a wave of popular enthusiasm for Maria Theresa. While Walpole still hoped for peace, the King and Parliament were for giving her all possible assistance. Britain, however, could do little to help the Queen of Hungary immediately. As usual, the strength of the army had been heavily reduced in peacetime, and many months would be needed to assemble a force strong enough to intervene effectively on the Continent. The navy was engaged in a difficult war with Spain, started against Walpole's wishes on the insistence of the city merchants, and now derisively called the War of Jenkin's Ear when the expected victories failed to materialize. When in January 1741, the Austrian ambassador asked for British help, the King would not give a positive commitment for Britain, though he assured the ambassador of his friendship for Maria Theresa, and promised to assist her with all Electoral forces and the Hessian and Danish auxiliaries in British pay.[33]

Recognizing the danger that France and other countries might enter the war against Austria, the British government tried to bring about a reconciliation between Frederick and Maria Theresa. In February 1741, the British ambassador to Vienna was instructed to tell the Austrian court that the King would use his good offices to arrange an accommodation with Frederick if desired; shortly afterwards the ambassador was ordered to put pressure on the Queen to accept the offer.[34] The Austrians' first reaction to this proposal was that the King's assistance would be welcome if it were made at the head of 25000 men, while Frederick, when he first heard of Britain's efforts in February, had been ready to accept mediation only if it were carried out with the utmost impartiality, i.e. if he obtained all he wanted. A month later, he declared himself ready to come to Austria's aid if he received Lower Silesia and Breslau, mentioning that he was as yet unengaged, in spite of having received advantageous proposals from France.[35] In April, after being defeated at Mollwitz by one of Frederick's generals, the Austrians were beginning to think of an accommodation with Prussia, when they were greatly heartened by the news that the British parliament was prepared to assist them.[36] Parliament granted Maria Theresa a subsidy of £300000, a considerable sum which, together with the loyalty of her subjects, enabled the Queen to defend herself. Foreseeing that British aid to Austria might endanger the Electorate, both Houses of Parliament, in April 1741, assured the King that they would defend any part of his dominions (i.e. Hanover) if attacked because of this British quarrel. Maria Theresa now informed her ambassador in London that she was not willing to accept mediation, but called on Britain and the Netherlands to fulfil their treaty obligations.[37] She would not give up any part of her inheritance, not even a small portion of Silesia to provide a corridor between Saxony and Poland, although the King-Elector was willing to assist her if she would cede it to him. Her refusal did not offend the British, and on 13/24 June, treaties of assistance between Austria and both Britain and Hanover were signed in London.

By now, France was ready to enter the war. She could not do so directly, as she had already recognized Maria Theresa as Queen of Hungary and Bohemia, but found a way out by calling herself an ally of Bavaria, whose Elector claimed the Austrian inheritance for his wife. On 4 June, France concluded an alliance with Prussia, guaranteeing Prussia's conquests in Silesia. The French now formed two armies, one to invade Austria and Bohemia, the other to march into northern Germany and threaten Hanover, while their allies, Spain and Savoy, attacked the Austrian dominions in Italy. On 15 July, Munchhausen summed up the political situation from his point of view. Admitting that the preservation of the House of Austria was in the interest of both Britain and Hanover, he reasoned that it was now too late for intervention with the armed forces of the Electorate. Three months ago, he had recommended maintaining the peace by uniting all forces against those who threatened it. Now war would only produce the ruin of his country. No ally could be expected to sacrifice himself in a hopeless cause, especially in view of Austria's obstinacy in refusing any accommodation with Prussia.[38]

King George, who was spending the summer in his Electorate, began to worry about its safety. He wrote to London asking whether neutrality in the coming struggle would be feasible. Newcastle, in a letter to Harrington, Secretary for the North, who had accompanied the King, replied that neutrality for England was impracticable, while neutrality for Hanover was not the ministers' concern. Vienna's obstinacy was not sufficient to discharge His Majesty of his obligations. The Danes and Hessians were to be dispatched to Maria Theresa to use as she thought fit. He suggested putting more pressure on the Queen, but without driving her into the hands of France. A fortnight later, he informed Harrington that there were 12000 men in England ready to sail for Germany to replace the Danes and Hessians.[39] Harrington answered that George felt Hanover was in great danger, and that the only way to save it would be to remain neutral as Elector. A few days later, he added that the Danes and Hessians in British pay could not be sent to the Queen of Hungary, as their presence in Hanover was absolutely essential. Besides, they would be of more service to Maria Theresa there than anywhere else, because they would bind a large number of Prussian troops.[40] Newcastle was highly indignant. 'Was there ever such a letter ... so little becoming an English minister?', he wrote to the Lord Chancellor.[41] In his reply to Harrington, he did not mention neutrality at all, but merely assured him that Britain would defend Hanover if attacked.

The King faced a difficult choice. As Elector of Hanover, he could not bring himself to expose his country to ruin by sending troops to aid Austria, whose cause already seemed hopeless; as King of Great Britain, he could not permit a country under his rule to join an enemy of Britain's ally. He was in anxiety and despair, and even thought of taking his own life rather than outlive the destruction of his Electorate.[42] At last, he sent an emissary to Paris to negotiate a neutrality agreement for Hanover. The French, who did not want to go to war with Britain, consented readily enough, and a gentlemen's agreement was concluded between the King of France and the Elector of Hanover, in which Louis XV undertook to leave Hanover alone against George's promise to vote for France's candidate in the coming Imperial election, the Elector of Bavaria.[43] Hanover was safe for the time being, though the French kept troops in Westfalia in case George should change his mind.

The treaty of assistance between Hanover and Austria had already been abrogated by George on the grounds that it had been based on the expectation that Saxony would fight on the Austrian side. Saxony had, however, made common cause with Prussia because the Austrians had refused to give her the corridor to Poland. Whether an Elector of Hanover with no ties to another country would now have joined the Prussians and Saxons in order to gain some additional territory, and whether this would have benefitted Hanover in the long run, is a question which posterity cannot answer.

The news that George as Elector had concluded a treaty of neutrality for Hanover was greeted with a torrent of abuse in England. The people said that evidently their little peacock of a King cared more for the safety of his miserable Electorate than for the honour of his kingdom.[44] In the House of Lords, the treaty was called shameful, dishonourable, and a betrayal of the public faith and the liberties of Europe, though the House finally accepted the ministry's claim that Hanover was a separate state and its affairs did not come under Parliamentary cognizance. Newcastle, who as a member of the government could not speak out in Parliament, was especially bitter about this 'fatal neutrality'. He refused to send the promised 12000 soldiers to the Electorate or to aid Hanover with money on the grounds that the King had refused to send the Danes and Hessians to Maria Theresa's aid.[45] He blamed Hanover for the dangerous situation Austria found herself in. Only Electoral jealousy of the King of Prussia had prevented an agreement between Frederick and the Queen of Hungary. For the same reason, the Dutch, Saxons and Russians had not been encouraged to come to the aid of the House of Austria. There was great uneasiness among His Majesty's faithful subjects.[46] Though Newcastle's accusations were hardly correct — the Russians were defending themselves against Sweden, instigated to attack them by France, the Saxons had been rebuffed by Austria, and the Dutch would only stir under strong British pressure — his opinion reflected popular feeling.

The Hanoverian ministers saw things differently. They complained that because of the King's leaning towards the Queen of Hungary, things had come to the point where all Hanoverian troops including the Danes and Hessians were required for the defence of the Electorate, as Maria Theresa was quite unable to give any help. They had foreseen this situation months ago, and were very sorry to see their predictions verified. They could not understand why the Electorate should be deprived of its foreign auxiliaries in favour of Austria, who by her obstinacy had brought her difficulties upon herself.[47]

Early in September, the Austrian ambassador reported that he had received £175000 from Britain as the first instalment of the promised £300000. Of this he had paid £50000 to George as Elector of Hanover on the basis of an agreement with Maria Theresa to reimburse him for expenses incurred on her behalf in Germany.[48] The extraordinary fact that the Elector of Hanover had pocketed one-sixth of the money granted by the King and Parliament of Britain for the support of the Queen of Hungary — and this after he had refused to assist her — was of course kept a secret. If it had become public knowledge, the consequences would have been incalculable. The King might even have been forced to retire to Hanover. It has been surmised that George had previously lent the £50000 to Maria Theresa,[49] but it is difficult to reconcile this charitable theory with the text of the ambassador's report and George's penurious character (see Chapter 5). A few years later, the same ambassador was to report that getting money out of the Hanover treasury was as hopeless as trying to seize the moon with one's teeth.[50] It is quite certain that the Queen would never have given as much as a penny to a prince who was not also King of Britain. What George did with the money is not known. Presumably he used it to recoup the sums he had had to disburse in warlike preparations, though this was hardly justified as every German prince had been forced to spend as much money as he could afford in order to defend himself in these troubled times. A year before, the Elector had spent the same amount in acquiring the fortress of Steinhorst from Denmark, much to the relief of his British ministers, who wanted friendship with Copenhagen, and had been worried by the hostile conduct of Hanover before the purchase. But at that time George cannot have foreseen this new windfall. In October 1744, he paid Saxony, who by then was allied with Vienna, £50000.[51] The money was intended to help her war effort, but was George merely acting as a faithful ally or under the threat of discovery? The second alternative seems more likely.

The British government continued its efforts at mediation with unabated vigour. The court of Vienna, at last frightened by the march of French and Bavarian troops into Bohemia in August, agreed that the British ambassador to Austria, Robinson, should be sent to Frederick's camp in Silesia in order to arrange a settlement. Rebuffed on his first visit because he had no credentials from the Queen, he returned a month later, only to be pitied by Podewils, the Prussian chief minister, because he had so little to offer. Three months earlier, Podewils remarked, his king might have taken Maria Theresa's part if he had been offered only Lower Silesia, but now it was too late.[52] Abruptly dismissed by Frederick,[53] Robinson returned to Vienna empty-handed.

Frederick, though, was growing uneasy about the political situation, always fearing that France might make common cause with Austria against him. Under pressure from Lord Hyndford, the new British ambassador to Berlin, he concluded the convention of Klein-Schnellendorf on 9 October 1741, in which he agreed to remain neutral against cession of nearly all Silesia. Only a few weeks later, after the Franco-Bavarian allies had taken Prague on 26 November, he again entered the war. Maria Theresa's cause seemed lost, but she managed to counterattack by entering Bavaria early in the new year, and forcing the French to retreat. With no support on their right flank, the French troops in Westfalia had to be withdrawn, relieving the Electorate from anxiety. Britain again pressed Austria to make up with Frederick, but Maria Theresa felt she now had the upper hand in Silesia, and remained obstinate. A victory by Frederick over her brother-in-law Charles of Lorraine at last persuaded her to give way, and on 28 July 1742, the Peace of Berlin was signed. Prussia gained most of Silesia and agreed to remain neutral.

The misfortunes of Austria and his approval of Hanoverian neutrality had contributed to Walpole's downfall in January 1742. British foreign policy was now in the hands of Lord Carteret, the man who had conducted the Stockholm negotiations in 1719. Carteret had a grander vision of British policy in Europe than Walpole had had. His aim was to form a coalition of powers against France and relegate Britain's great rival to the second place once and for all. Especially, Germany under the new Bavarian Emperor Charles VII must not fall under French influence.

One of Carteret's first actions after taking office was to tell the Hanoverian minister in London that peace and quietness now reigned in Britain, and the King could ask for anything from his people. This *heure de berger* could be profitably exploited for foreign policy. France must be contained, for if she should achieve her aims on the Continent, it would soon be England's turn to submit to her. The Netherlands should be asked for active assistance against the French, and the same was true of the King of Prussia, for he was a man of importance and of excellent quality. The distinction between His Majesty as King and as Elector ought to be abolished, because the entire nation considered all his territories as their own. He proposed to visit the German Chancery that evening to be informed about the neutrality negotiations.[54]

Britain now began to take a more active part on the Continent. In April a force of 16000 men was sent to Flanders in order to deter France from attacking in the north and to encourage the Netherlands to come to Austria's assistance. Strong pressure was put on Austria to win over the King of Sardinia (Savoy) to her side by giving him a slice of the Austrian Milanese.[55] Maria Theresa very reluctantly agreed to cede part of her most valuable province, and only in the hope of obtaining Bavaria, a hope which was to be disappointed. The King of Sardinia, who did not mind balancing between France and Austria, but was afraid of Spain's return to Italy, was further granted a lavish British subsidy. He was at last persuaded to change sides, and the Austrians were relieved from defending their south. The Prussian King, also heard much stronger language from Carteret than he had been accustomed to. Hyndford was instructed to tell the Prussian court that Britain would stand by the House of Austria to the utmost of her power. King George would not be deterred from his alliance by threats to him either as King or as Elector. If France succeeded in destroying the Empire, Prussia's turn would come next.[56]

Frederick did not care to antagonize Britain, and signed the Treaty of Berlin, but not without asking for an assurance of British assistance in case he was attacked by the French in revenge for his accommodation with Maria Theresa, an assurance that was readily given.[57] In November 1742, the two countries concluded a defensive alliance at Westminster, though Frederick was not happy about it. He wrote to Podewils that he was signing the treaty à contre-coeur and if the British did not satisfy his interests, they would be the dupes.[58] However, without the alliance, as Podewils had told his master, Prussia would have stood alone. The ink was scarcely dry on the Treaty of Westminster, when Frederick began to threaten Hanover again. He told Hyndford that he did not mind if the English troops assembled in the Low Countries entered France, but if they crossed the Rhine into Germany, he must oppose them to protect the Emperor. The ambassador was not impressed. Though he could not counter the monarch directly, Hyndford told Podewils that: 'altho' the King my master is a younger Elector than Brandenburg, I would have you remember, Sir, that he is a much greater King.' If the Prussians wanted to quarrel, the question would be who had the longest purse as well as the longest sword. Nobody in Germany, he added, would prefer a Prussian army to an English one after the cruelties the Prussians had perpetrated the year before.[59] This was enough to end Frederick's threats.

By now, Hanoverian neutrality had ended. In February 1742, the Electoral ministers had advised the King that he could not aid Austria without needlessly sacrificing his country and his people. A month later, they counselled him not to renew the neutrality agreement on the grounds that such an agreement already existed, but applied only to Germany. If it were renewed, the French would insist on extending it to all Europe, and Hanoverian troops would not be able to fight as British auxiliaries.[60] The change of heart was due to the influence of Carteret. Newcastle, Carteret's enemy, acknowledged that putting an end to Hanoverian neutrality was the best thing he had ever done.[61] The Electoral envoy, who had again been sent to Paris to renew the neutrality pact, was recalled. Now the French were suddenly eager to conclude a written convention, but the King allowed neutrality to lapse.

In July 1742, the King ordered 16 000 Hanoverians and 6 000 Hessians in British pay to march to Flanders, instructing Carteret that care should be taken to provide them with proper quarters, sustenance and forage. A general was sent from London to field headquarters to make sure these particulars were attended to.[62] The British commander in Flanders, Lord Stair, was in high hopes. As soon as the Hanoverians and Hessians arrived, he expected to take the combined army into Northern France, and even thought of occupying Paris. He was to be disappointed. The movements of the Germans were 'most unaccountably slow', although everything had been prepared for them on their marching route. In spite of Stair's mounting impatience, they did not reach his camp until the middle of October.[63] By then it was too late to begin a campaign, and the army spent an inactive winter in its quarters. The reasons for the delay in the Hanoverians' arrival are not known. Many suspected at the time that the King was trying to spare his Electoral troops, but there is no proof of this. It is more probable that they were held up by the weather. The autumn of 1742 was unusually rainy and the roads were hardly passable. Stair might not have been able to march into France even if he had assembled his army in time.

The King had told his British ministers that as Elector he could not afford to keep so many soldiers in the field, and they agreed to take them into British pay, and even accorded them much better conditions than his father's troops had received in 1702.[64] The money had to be granted by Parliament, and a lively debate ensued when the proposal was put forward in December 1742. Opponents asserted that the undertaking to pay the Electoral army by Britain was made only in the interests of Hanover, that British policy since George I had always been subservient to the wishes of that territory, and that the Hanoverians were resting in Flanders, doing nothing. Pitt, on behalf of the opposition, made a speech in which he declared that 'this great, this powerful, this formidable kingdom is now considered only a province to a despicable Electorate'. The government, on the other hand, pointed out that Hanoverian troops were particularly reliable, being subjects of the same prince as Britons, and that Hanoverian troops were as cheap and as good as any forces that could be obtained elsewhere. The motion to take them into British pay was adopted by 260 votes to 198 in the Commons, and by 90 to 35 in the Lords.

It was only in the spring of 1743 that the so-called Pragmatic Army in Flanders was able to set out for the South. Besides the troops already mentioned, it was reinforced by Dutch and Austrian contingents. By June, it was encamped near Aschaffenburg on the Main, and there it was joined by King George. A few days afterwards, it fought the battle of Dettingen, gaining a narrow victory. The allies had manoeuvred themselves into a tight corner and were almost beaten by the French. Only the bravery of the soldiers, together with some indiscipline on the part of the enemy, saved the day. George personally took part in the fighting — his hat was shot off — and it may well have been the presence of their monarch which inspired the British and Hanoverians and proved to be the decisive factor. Rumour has it that George ordered the British into battle with the cry: 'Now fight for de honour of England, charge!'[65] Dettingen was not a decisive victory, but it stopped French progress along the valley of the Main, and forced the enemy to retreat across the Rhine. There they could not be pursued, for it was difficult to cross the marshy banks of the river against opposition without adequate preparations. The news of the battle was received with great acclaim in England, and Handel composed his Dettingen *Te Deum* for the occasion. But the triumph was short-lived.

Aversion to the Hanover connection had been growing ever since the declaration of neutrality in 1741. Now reports came in of the King's partiality towards his Hanoverians. While the Hanoverians had received all the bread and forage they needed, British troops had been left to starve. The King had consulted only Electoral officers, while no British officer had been permitted access to him. The British had had to bear the brunt of the battle, while the Germans stayed safely in the rear. Much was made of the fact that the King had worn a yellow Hanoverian sash on the day of the battle (the British sash was red), and Lord Stair was said to have resigned his command on the day after the battle. There seems to be little substance in these allegations apart from the inevitable petty squabbles between allies and the indubitable determination of the King that the Hanoverians should receive the same treatment as the British. The British, as members of the more powerful nation felt a perhaps natural jealousy at having to share the attention of their monarch with soldiers of a much less important country. Lord Stair did indeed resign, but only two months after Dettingen, it being generally agreed that there were faults on both sides.[66] Only a few days before the battle, he had gone out of his way to commend the bravery of the Electoral troops.[67] As to the King's partiality, even the Duke of Richmond, a decided opponent of the Hanoverians, acknowledged that George had spent as much time at the head of the British troops at Dettingen, as he had at the head of the Hanoverians.[68]

The Parliamentary opposition did not bother to examine

such details. Advantage was taken of the popular discontent to table motions both in the Lords and in the Commons requesting that the Hanoverians be dismissed from the British service. It was claimed that they were cowardly, disobedient, insolent, mercenaries and slaves. They came from a wretched corner of the earth, scarcely heard of until their sovereign was raised to the throne of Great Britain. They had enjoyed all comforts, while British troops, composed of free men, were treated with contempt. They were grossly overpaid at six pence a day. It was better for Britain to be made a province of France than to be subject to a despicable and dependent Electorate.[69]

The government denied the allegations against the Hanoverians and pointed out that the casualty lists showed that they had fought as bravely as the British, that no other troops were to be had, and that Britain might lose the war without these dependable soldiers. But many of the country gentlemen who usually voted with the government were unimpressed and sided with the opposition. Although the motion to dismiss the Electoral troops was voted down in both Houses, ministers chose not to risk another debate. During the following year, the Hanoverians were transferred to the service of Maria Theresa, additional subsidies being granted for the purpose. A treaty was made between His British Majesty and the Queen in which she undertook to pay the additional £200000 allotted to her to the person authorized by His Majesty in his quality as Elector, on condition that his German troops were employed in the Low Countries.[70]

Carteret continued with his policy of uniting Europe against France. His treaty of Hanau, in August 1743, was designed to detach the Bavarian Emperor from his alliance with France, but was not ratified in Britain because Charles VII demanded too heavy a subsidy, besides territorial acquisitions to support his Imperial dignity. The treaty of Worms, in September, which brought Austria, Holland, Saxony, and Sardinia (Savoy) into an alliance with Britain was accepted by the cabinet, but only with difficulty. A serious consequence of the treaty of Worms was that it aroused the suspicions of Frederick of Prussia, who began to fear that the Emperor might be deposed, and that he would be left to face Austria and the Empire without allies. He was even more afraid that France, which had been invaded by the Austrian army in the spring of 1744, might make peace with Maria Theresa and join forces with her against Prussia. Not without some difficulty, he managed to come to an understanding with Louis XV, and persuade him to declare war against both Britain and Austria.[71] A Franco-Prussian alliance was concluded in June 1744, and in August, Frederick again entered the war, proclaiming in a manifesto that one of his major reasons for doing so was the improper treatment of the Emperor by the British.[72] The Prussian army advanced into Bohemia, and took the city of Prague, forcing Maria Theresa to abandon the invasion of France and concentrate on the defence of her eastern territories.

Shortly after signing his treaty with France, Frederick had suggested to Paris that the French could not give George a more mortal blow than by sending a body of 20000 to 30000 men to invade Hanover, George would then immediately begin to talk of peace or neutrality. At the least, he would have to cease all aid to the Queen of Hungary.[73] The French made preparations for an attack on the Electorate in 1745, and even thought of giving Bremen and Verden to Denmark,[74] but these plans were given up. When Britain had invoked the treaty of Westminster and asked for Prussian aid against France, Frederick had refused to help on the grounds that Britain was the aggressor. But when things went badly for him in Bohemia, he had no hesitation about claiming the British guarantee for Silesia.[75]

Carteret now devised a grand scheme of uniting Britain, Austria, the Netherlands, Saxony-Poland, and Russia against all enemies,[76] but had no success because Austria wanted to direct her main attack against Prussia instead of France, as Carteret wanted. The Russians were struggling with internal difficulties and could not join. The failure of his European policy contributed to Carteret's downfall early in 1745. His colleagues had always found his overbearing manner hard to stomach and were now worried about being accused of making British interests subservient to those of Hanover.[77] Foreign policy was again directed by Newcastle. At about the same time, the Bavarian Emperor died, suddenly, but conveniently for almost everybody.

The Prussian King now wanted peace. He had learned that he could not make further conquests in Bohemia, and after the Emperor's death he could no longer hope to find allies within the Empire. He only wanted to keep what he had got, especially because he still feared that Austria might come to an arrangement with France and would then be free to direct all her efforts against Prussia. Those fears were not unfounded, for if they had to choose between their two enemies, Maria Theresa, King George, and the Hanoverians would all have preferred a settlement with France.[78] The British cabinet, however, saw France as the main enemy and was adamant. Harrington, who had again travelled to Hanover with the King, was ordered to obtain His Majesty's consent to a treaty with Prussia. A reduction of Prussia, he was told, was indeed desirable, but a continuance of the war would only make her king more powerful. If Frederick's 100000 men were taken out of the scale, the allies might make headway against France. 'We must get this thorn out of our sides.'[79] Reluctantly, the King gave way and on 25 August 1745, the Convention of Hanover was signed. Frederick promised to cease hostilities on condition Britain pressed Maria Theresa to do the same, and Britain guaranteed his possession of Silesia.

Robinson was now instructed to use his 'utmost endeavour' to prevail upon Maria Theresa to end her war with Prussia. A fortnight later, he was ordered to renew his efforts 'in the most pressing manner' and 'with all zeal and earnestness'. She was to be told that the war in Flanders was going badly, and that the King of Sardinia urgently needed succour which the Austrians could not send while their troops were tied up in Bohemia. Maria Theresa was not to be moved. In spite of two victories by Frederick, she still believed she could defeat him and was in fact pressing him hard. She persisted in her '*d e v i l i s h*' obstinacy, as the despairing Robinson described it,[80] until the combined Austro-Saxon army lost the battle of Kesselsdorf in December, and Saxony was no longer able to continue the war. Peace with Prussia was concluded at Dresden on 25 December 1745. Frederick kept Silesia and promised to recognize Maria Theresa's husband as Emperor.

Earlier in the year, Britain had been attacked from the rear when Prince Charles Stuart landed in Scotland and started a rebellion. The government recalled British troops, aided by Dutch regiments, from Flanders. As in 1715, no Hanoverian soldiers were asked to assist their monarch because of the political dangers involved, but the Hanoverians now had to bear a larger share of the fighting in Flanders. Only a year after they had left the British service, their soldiers were taken back into British pay, Parliament voting 255 to 122 in favour of the measure. Pitt had been made vice-treasurer of Ireland, and held his peace.[81]

The war between Britain and France dragged on for another three years. While the British were victorious at sea, the French armies advanced relentlessly in Flanders. When both sides were exhausted by the war, peace was concluded at Aachen (Aix-la-Chapelle) in 1748. As Spain wanted to obtain some advantage for herself after the years of fighting, Maria Theresa had to be bullied into ceding the Duchy of Parma to a Spanish Infant. Otherwise, the peace was based on the principle of returning all conquests made during the war, greatly disappointing the American colonists, who had to give up the island of Cape Breton which they had taken almost without assistance from the mother country. Hanover got nothing, though she had borne a considerable share of the fighting (but none of the expense) during the war. The only real victor was Frederick of Prussia, who had gained a valuable province, and had established his country as a rival to Austria in the Empire. Maria Theresa had managed to keep the bulk of her inheritance intact, but grieved over the loss of Silesia and territories in Italy, for which she blamed her British allies more than her enemies.

The general feeling was that the peace was no more than a stalemate, the French naming it *la paix bête*. There could be little doubt that hostilities would recommence as soon as one of the parties had recovered sufficiently to hope for victory. Maria Theresa wanted to regain Silesia, while

Britain and France would continue to quarrel over their
trade and their overseas dominions.

7

THE SEVEN YEARS' WAR

During the first years after the peace treaty, Britain was governed by the Pelham administration, with Henry Pelham as First Lord of the Treasury — in effect Prime Minister — and his brother the Duke of Newcastle in charge of foreign affairs, while Pitt was appointed paymaster of the Forces and ceased to be a thorn in the ministry's side. Pelham's main concern was the restoration of the country's economy after the long war. He put financial affairs in order and carried out several mild reforms. His determination to economize included the army and the navy, both of which were reduced to a margin that proved to be dangerously low when war came.

In 1748, Newcastle visited Hanover with the King and was quite taken in by its delights.[1] He formed a personal friendship with von Munchhausen which extended to their wives, and for the rest of the period in office kept up a regular correspondence with him.[2] The Duke conceived the idea of forging closer ties with Maria Theresa for both Britain and Hanover by bringing about the election of her son as King of the Romans, an election which would have ensured his succession to the Imperial throne on his father's death. In spite of Pelham's opposition, much British money was spent on bribing various Electors to accede to the proposal, but their collective demands were too high. In 1753, the Imperial court, which had been lukewarm all along, politely rejected the plan.[3]

After only five years of peace, there were signs of another rupture between Britain and France. Apart from Britons' fears that their trade might be eclipsed by the French, there were differences over the two countries' colonies in America, Africa, and India. The situation was especially tense in North America, where English-speaking settlers from the relatively thickly populated Atlantic seaboard were pressing over the ill-defined Appalachian frontier into lands claimed by France, but inhabited only by a few Indian tribes. The first shots were fired there in 1754, followed by naval action in the Atlantic, but neither country was ready to declare war.

The British government was worried about the fate of Hanover if the French were to occupy it during hostilities, not only because Hanover belonged to their monarch, and would have to be redeemed at the end of a war, but also because the Electorate, with the duchies of Bremen and Verden, controlled the entry ports for British trade with Germany. At first, approaches were made to Britain's traditional friend, Austria, but the Austrians would only enter into an alliance if they were promised the recovery of Silesia, or at least an equivalent. This was a condition the government could not agree to. Britain's guarantee of the possession of Silesia to Prussia might indeed have been declared void because Prussia had in the meantime become an ally of Britain's enemy France. A war against Prussia would, however, bring about the very situation Britain was trying to avoid, i.e. the occupation of the Electorate by enemy forces. Even if Russia came to Austria's aid, the defence of Hanover against Prussia would require the deployment of far more troops than Britain had at her disposal or could train within a reasonable time, especially as the money would have to be granted by Parliament. Parliament would never sanction supplies for a war of aggression against Prussia, and even if it did, the debates would become known to the public and thus to the Prussian King, who would make a preventive attack long before preparations could be completed. The British ambassador to Vienna was therefore told that the King would never enter into so unjust and impracticable a project as an attack on Prussia, which might be beneficial to Austria, but could produce no solid advantage to His Majesty, though if Prussia should attack Austria, His Majesty would not forget his attachment to his old and natural allies and come to their aid.[4]

Britain now turned her attention towards Prussia. If Frederick could be persuaded to remain neutral during the coming conflict with France, Hanover's eastern frontier would be safe, and there would be time to ward off a French invasion if it came. Relations with Prussia were not good, however. When Frederick had annexed Silesia, he had acknowledged a British loan made to the province when it was still Austrian, and had regularly serviced the debt. In 1752, he suddenly refused to pay the instalment then due, on the grounds that he claimed compensation for losses suffered by his merchantmen at the hands of British privateers during the last war, a claim that may have been justified, for the British ambassador to Berlin reported that he believed that the privateers' conduct had fallen little short of downright piracy.[5] The news of Frederick's default was followed by disquieting rumours from Berlin. British malcontents were received in Prussia with open arms and there was talk of assisting the Pretender. During the winter of 1751/52, there was great alarm in Hanover, as a Prussian invasion was thought imminent. The King ordered preparations to be made for defence. Munchhausen was the only one to keep a cool head amid the general consternation. He wrote to the King that Prussia could do nothing without France, and that France was not yet ready to start a general war. While there was no danger at present, he suggested that further threats could be taken care of by seeking an agreement with Russia, as only fear of Russia could keep Frederick in check.[6]

In 1753 the British government, perhaps because the King had passed on Munchhausen's suggestion, began to negotiate with Russia about a defensive treaty, i.e. a treaty meant to restrain Prussia from attacking Hanover. At first, no agreement was reached because Russia demanded subsidies even in peacetime. These Pelham was not willing to grant, partly out of fear of stirring up another storm about Hanover in Parliament.[7] In 1754 Pelham died, and Newcastle took over the reins of government. Now it was possible to come to an arrangement which would satisfy St. Petersburg. Against payment of an annual subsidy of £100000, to be increased to £500000 if war should break out, the Russians undertook to station 55000 troops in Livonia. This army was to be used only in Germany, and only if Britain or her allies (i.e. Hanover) were attacked.

Until now, all attempts to come to an understanding with Prussia had been unsuccessful. In 1755, Holdernesse, then Secretary of State for the North, had asked the Duke of Brunswick (there had been no British ambassador to Berlin for years) to inform Frederick that Britain would like a declaration from him that he would not hinder George II in the defence of Hanover. Frederick told the Duke that he was ready to amuse Britain with negotiations, but at the same time assured him that he would never give such a declaration. *Ce fichu pays* wanted him to espouse its interests while their differences were unresolved. If England were to make clear proposals, he would answer. But he was resolved not to give up France for the glory of having preserved Hanover, a country of no interest to him.[8] He did not inform the Duke that, only a short time before, he had ordered his envoy in Paris to insinuate to the French ministry that if England wished to start a general war, he could send a considerable body of troops into Hanover and force George to re-establish peace.[9] When, in October, the Hanover ministry asked him for help in case of a possible French invasion, he gave a polite but vague answer.[10]

After the Anglo-Russian convention had been signed at St. Petersburg in September 1755, the British government informed the Prussian ambassador about it, and explained that the treaty was merely a defensive one. Britain did not wish to involve anyone in her quarrel with France, and believed that Prussia held the key to peace in Europe. She was ready to come to an agreement with Frederick that included the settlement of all outstanding differences and a guarantee for Silesia. Frederick, who feared nothing more than a Russian attack, declared that he received the news with pleasure and professed himself ready to conclude a treaty of neutrality for Germany.[11] The convention of Westminster between the two countries was signed on 16 January 1756, providing for the neutrality of Germany during a war between Britain and France, and armed resistance to any foreign troops which attempted to enter or pass through any German territory, the Austrian Netherlands specifically excepted. The matter of the Silesian loan was settled by a compromise, and full diplomatic relations were resumed.

The treaties with both St Petersburg and Berlin were approved by Parliament. When the Russian treaty and one with Hesse were brought before the Commons on 10 December, Pitt protested that they were purely in defence of Hanover, and that 'we are pressed into the service of an Electorate'. His speech, which led to his dismissal from government service, left the ministers unmoved. They declared that the treaties would be necessary even if there were no connection between Britain and Hanover, because they would prevent the French from forcing the Austrians or the Dutch to enter the war against Britain. Hanover was a topic which would always be used by the disaffected for raising distrust against the ruling House among the populace, but Hanover must be defended like any other ally.

When the treaty with Prussia was brought before the House on 11 May 1756, Pitt, now in opposition, attacked it even more bitterly. While he admitted that Hanover could not be neglected, and must be indemnified for any damage when peace was restored, he considered that country indefensible. He ardently wished to break the fetters that bound Britain to that barren rock. Hanover was a territory so inconsiderable that its name could not be found on any map. His oratory came too late to have any effect.

In November 1755, in the face of imminent war with France, Parliament had already voted large supplies for the armed forces, and at the same time assured the King that all his dominions, even though not belonging to the Crown of Great Britain (i.e. Hanover) would be defended in this British quarrel. The resolution was adopted by a huge majority in the Commons. In the Lords, there was no division, though the motion had been opposed on the grounds that a promise to defend Hanover would only incite the enemy to attack it, and — somewhat contradictorily — that only self-preservation would hinder Britain from defending the Electorate. In March of the following year (1756), both Houses, frightened at the prospect of a French invasion, had 'beseeched' the King to order twelve battalions of his Electoral troops to England in order to defend the kingdom. Pitt thought this unnecessary, but was outvoted by 259 to 92. The King, giving his Hanoverian ministers only a fortnight to make the necessary preparations, commanded the troops to be sent over. They spent the summer and autumn in the south of England, but were sent home shortly after Pitt became prime minister (and there had been time to put Britain's defences in order).

The treaty between Britain and Prussia had been intended by both sides to keep Germany at peace. George sent a letter to all the Princes of the Empire explaining that both parties only meant to maintain peace within the Empire and that he had vainly asked for the assistance of the Imperial court. He was also at pains to allay the fears of the Roman Catholic Princes that it might be directed against them.[12] Frederick similarly informed all Prussian envoys that his treaty with the English Crown had no other purpose than that of keeping Germany out of the war between England and France. He also wrote a confidential letter to his representative in Paris stating that only necessity had forced him to conclude the treaty offered by the English, especially as a French attack on Hanover had no chance of success after the Anglo-Russian convention.[13] Neither Britain nor Prussia suspected that the treaty would serve to bring war on the Continent nearer.

The first to react was Elizabeth of Russia. Elizabeth disliked Frederick politically because she did not want a strong power near her western borders. But she hated him deeply for personal reasons because he dared to make public fun of her amours, although all Europe knew he was a homosexual. Only two days after she had ratified the Anglo-Russian convention, she received news of the treaty with Prussia, and did not bother to conceal her disappointment to the British ambassador.[14] She did not abrogate her treaty with Britain — after all, she could always do with a subsidy — but it soon became clear that she wanted to fight no one but Prussia.

The court of Versailles also took offence at the Convention

of Westminster. France had regarded Prussia as a client state, and had been ready to renew her alliance with Berlin. Now Prussia had signed a treaty with France's enemy, while her value as an ally had been much reduced by Britain's convention with the Tsarina. France was now ready to listen to proposals from Austria, where Chancellor Kaunitz had been pressing for an alliance for many years. On 1 May 1756, the two countries signed a treaty that was of a purely defensive nature, as Maria Theresa was not yet ready to break with Britain, the only country that had helped her when she was fighting to save her inheritance. But the treaty alarmed Frederick, who in March had been looking forward to renewing his alliance with France. Now that Versailles and Vienna were united, he was no longer willing to do so.[15]

As soon as she was sure that France would not come to the aid of Prussia, Maria Theresa began to negotiate in earnest with Elizabeth and the King-Elector of Saxony-Poland about a joint attack on Frederick. Hostilities were to begin in 1757, as time was needed to make preparations. If possible, France was to join in the fighting, and Kaunitz went so far as to promise her the cession of the Austrian Netherlands if Silesia were regained. Frederick was informed about these plans through a traitor at the Saxon court[16] and decided on a preventive strike. At the end of August 1756, he marched his army into Saxony in the hope that he would eliminate one of his potential enemies and break up the coalition of the others before it was completed. The attack on Saxony was successful, partly because the King-Elector and his powerful Chief Minister, Count Bruhl, had preferred to spend British subsidies on embellishing the capital city of Dresden instead of using them to build up the army.

Frederick's success was, however, only a local one. While he could press the Saxon troops into his service, and plunder the country's resources to finance his war, Maria Theresa could now invoke her defensive treaty with France. Versailles joined the Russo-Austrian alliance and promised to send troops and subsidies. The Empire, with only a few dissenting voices, declared itself against Prussia, and even Sweden was forced into the war. The real fight began in the following year.[17]

George as Elector did his best to keep Hanover neutral. He made it clear to everyone that the Electorate had no part in the quarrel between the Empress-Queen and the King of Prussia, and that any warlike preparations he was making were only for defence if Hanover were to be attacked.[18] He began to negotiate with Austria about a treaty of neutrality. The Austrians were willing to agree to this, but needed the consent of their French allies, who wanted to impose strict conditions. George's British ministers knew about these talks, and informed him that while they could have no objection to Electoral neutrality, he should not compromise his honour, i.e. they advised him that Hanover must not be permitted to help Prussia's enemies. At length, the Austrian ambassador in London presented the final draft of a neutrality agreement to the King in April 1757. Its chief provisions were: the right of 'innocuous transit' for the French armies through the Electorate; the obligation to furnish provisions and forage against payment; and the cession of the fortress of Hamelin to the French for the duration of hostilities. It was evident that this sort of neutrality was not neutrality at all, but meant the furnishing of active aid to one of the contending parties. If it had been accepted, Frederick would have been perfectly justified in invading and occupying Hanover without warning, not to speak of the highly unfavourable reaction in Britain. George told the ambassador that he could not accept the proposal, and informed his Hanoverian ministers accordingly.[19]

Strange to say, the ministers did not share their monarch's opinion. Instead of beginning active preparations for the now inevitable armed struggle, they made what delays they could. Not only did they refuse to send troops to strengthen the Prussian fortress of Wesel on the Rhine, as Frederick wanted them to do, but they prevented the passage of Prussian troops to Wesel under the pretext that no specific orders had been received from London. Contractors for the army were told that they need not be in a hurry with their deliveries, and horses continued to be sold as remounts for the Austrian cavalry.

The Prussian King was beside himself with indignation.

He complained that he was being betrayed by the very people he had saved, and that the *perruques d'Hanovre*, as he described the ministers, were both helpless and obstinate. He had sent his general von Schmettau to Hanover to report on the preparations for war, and Schmettau had found them totally insufficient. For example, only 100 waggons had been provided for 30000 troops, while everybody knew that 700 were required.[20] Frederick insisted that the Duke of Cumberland be sent to command the Hanoverian army as no one else would have the authority to deal with the recalcitrant ministers. The comments made by Mitchell, the British ambassador to Berlin, after a visit to Hanover were even more scathing: 'the best thing I can say for the Hanoverian ministry is their incapacity . . . their duplicity and low cunning is not to be described . . . I am quite tired of their shuffling and indirect manner . . . it is with the greatest veracity that I can say they are become the scorn and reproach of Germany . . . they are all at heart Austrians'.[21] There is nothing in the Hanover archives to dispel the impression that the ministers' conduct was dilatory, to say the least.[22] They hated and feared Prussia, and were probably convinced that Frederick must succumb to his many and powerful enemies. Accordingly, they wished to remain on good terms with the victors. Their attitude did not improve until, early in 1758, George sent strict orders to his ministers to adhere to his political system, reminding them of their oath of office and threatening his personal displeasure if one of them failed in his duty.

In the spring of 1757, the French army crossed the Rhine and advanced towards Hanover. It consisted of 80000 men, but was poorly disciplined and encumbered with baggage and camp-followers. The Hanoverian forces, under the Duke of Cumberland, with the addition of Hessian and Brunswick detachments, amounted to 30000-40000 troops. Parliament, under Pitt's first premiership, had granted £200000 for their maintenance and supplies. The ensuing battle of Hastenbeck (26 July 1757) might have been won by the Hanoverians, but Cumberland ordered a premature retreat. Instead of withdrawing towards Prussia, he sought the safety of the fortress of Stade on the Elbe, and the greater part of the Electorate was overrun by the French, who were now able to spare 20000 men to send to their armies in the south.

The King received the news of the defeat of Hastenbeck calmly. He ordered his son to arrange the best terms he could with the French, on condition his troops were not disarmed, and instructed his Electoral envoy at Vienna to ask for a separate peace. As he wrote to the envoy, he had never had any part in the quarrel between the Houses of Austria and Brandenburg. He had been compelled to fight, but divine providence had not blessed his arms and he must now give way to force. All he wanted was to free his lands from trouble, though he must not be obliged to act against the King of Prussia. The British ministers knew about these negotiations, but felt powerless to intervene.[23] However, they assured Frederick, who had made strong complaints, that the overtures made by the Electoral ministers would not have the least influence on the conduct of His Majesty as King of Great Britain.[24]

The Austrians were not unwilling to come to an arrangement, and might even have consented to release George from his Electoral duty to furnish troops to the Empire if they were well paid for such a concession. The King was in fact ready to disburse a 'considerable sum' if his German territories were freed from occupation before winter. Evidently, as Elector of Hanover, he saw no inconsistency in furnishing Prussia's enemy with money that would be used in the war against his ally as King of Britain. If such a thought did cross his mind, he may have reflected that no part of the amount would reach Britain's enemy, France. Of course, such an argument would not have saved him from the storm of reproach that would have arisen in Britain if he had made the payment. Perhaps fortunately for the Hanoverian dynasty, the French commander, the Duc de Richelieu, would not consent to any settlement. Neutrality had been offered and refused. He must now look to the interests of the allies and the glory of His Most Christian Majesty.[25] On 8 September 1757, Cumberland and Richelieu concluded the Convention of Kloster Zeven, according to which all Hanover, with the exception of Stade and Lauenburg, was to be occupied by the French. All George's hopes for saving his Electorate were destroyed.

Furious, he declared he was bound hand and foot to France. He had lost his honour and was absolutely undone. Speaking of his son, he declared: 'a scoundrel in England one day may be thought a good man another, in Germany it is otherwise; I think like a German'.[26] The Duke of Cumberland was too proud to defend himself, and retired from the court. He might have answered that he had acted under necessity, had not exceeded his father's orders — in this he was supported by Pitt — and that in view of the geographical situation of the Electorate, it was not possible for it to remain aloof from a war between the great powers.

The French proceeded to plunder Hanover at their leisure, with the ill-disciplined troops committing many excesses. Richelieu did so well for himself that he was able to build a palace in Paris which for many years was dubbed the 'Palais d'Hanovre' by the wits. Only the town of Hanover itself was somewhat spared, the local commander, the Duc de Randau, being a just and honest man who managed to keep his troops in check.[27]

In spite of his mistrust of the Hanoverian ministers, Frederick had thought it incredible that they could set their hands to a convention of neutrality. When he heard that the 'dishonourable and ignominious' convention had actually been signed, he blamed the fact on the ministers' pernicious influence on the Duke of Cumberland and wondered whether he was not entitled to take reprisals against this act of treachery.[28] He urged George to repudiate the convention because it had been broken by the French.[29] The British ministers were of the same opinion. They pointed out that the French had violated the convention by demanding that the Hessian auxiliaries be disarmed. 'H.M.'s English servants, though they did not dare to presume to offer advice in regard to the affairs of the Electorate, yet thought it their duty . . .' to tell the King that they were ready to support him if, on the advice of his Electoral ministers, he considered the convention no longer binding, but that it was impossible to give succour while the Electoral troops remained inactive.[30] The King received no such advice from his Hanoverian ministers, who were afraid of drawing the wrath of France on their country. But after the Prussian army had inflicted a crushing defeat on the

French and their Imperial allies at Rossbach on 5 November, he felt free to act and orders were sent to the troops at Stade to resume hostilities.

In spite of Richelieu's threat to destroy the Electorate and his order to confiscate the property of all Hanoverian officers, the allies advanced against the retreating French, and soon the country was free again. Energetic measures were now taken to prevent a renewed invasion. The Hanoverian soldiers were taken into British pay, and considerable British forces were sent over to assist them. One of Frederick's generals, Ferdinand of Brunswick, was appointed Commander-in-Chief at the age of 36. During the following years, Ferdinand's army, with varying fortunes, managed to hold back the French and protect Frederick's western flank. Ferdinand's victory at Minden on 1 August 1759 may have a claim to be the world's most forgotten decisive battle. Without it Frederick would never have survived his disastrous defeat by the Russians at Kunersdorf a few days later. Minden receives only bare mention in German histories, where interest is centred on Frederick. In Britain it is somewhat better known because of the story of Lord Sackville's disobedience, and because the name is inscribed on monuments and regimental battle honours, but hardly anybody is aware of its importance.

From 1757 onwards, Frederick received British subsidies. He had at first believed that he could do without financial assistance, and had merely asked for a naval squadron to defend his Baltic ports against the Russians, a request that had met only evasive answers. After the failure of his invasion of Bohemia in the summer, he sent word that he needed a subsidy of 4 million Reichstalers (£800000-900000), a sum that surprised even his friend Mitchell. Under Pitt's second premiership, an agreement for the payment of this amount was concluded, and renewed annually. Frederick was enabled to hold out against his enemies. He was assisted by occasional British raids on the coast of France, which forced the French to keep a considerable number of their troops at home.

Britain had become involved in a full-scale war on the continent because she wanted to protect her King's native land, and the Hanoverian connection has been accused of causing an unnecessary loss of blood and treasure. It may, however, be doubted whether things would have turned out very differently if the King of Britain had not also been Elector of Hanover. Britain was at war with France over the possession of colonial territories. As the French could not hope to beat the British at sea, it seems quite probable that they would in any case have attempted to cut off their enemies from their markets by occupying the North Sea coast, and thus destroying their trade. The only way to prevent this would have been for Britain to seek allies on the Continent who would be able to keep the French out of north Germany, something the Austrians and Russians could not have done if Prussia had joined forces with France.

The ageing King wanted a compensation for the damage done to his native country and hoped for the addition of a province or two when peace came. Nowadays we may wonder how an increase of territory might have indemnified the inhabitants of the Electorate for the losses they had suffered at the hands of the French, but no such thought seems to have troubled eighteenth-century politicians. George kept pestering and cajoling his British ministers about a *dédommagement* for Hanover until they were tired of the subject. He said all he wanted was an assurance that at the peace conference which would end the war, the British delegates would support the representative of the Electorate; if no definite promises could be given, they might at least give him some hopes. Newcastle, in agreement with the rest of the cabinet, assured the King that no one was more devoted to his service than he. George's interests as king and Elector need not clash, but if they did, his royal ministers must see to it that his interests as king prevailed. The point of the matter was that Parliament would believe that any acquisition for the Electorate would be a diminution of the advantages which might have been procured for England. This circumlocutory way of saying that Hanover was a satellite state whose wishes need not be taken into account infuriated the King. 'You are all alike', he said, 'you will do nothing for me. You are thought the most ungrateful country thro'out Germany ... I will not trouble you anymore upon the subject ... I will let you do as you please this winter and leave you ...' (for Hanover).[31]

Undeterred by Newcastle's rebuff, the King ordered his German ministers to make plans for the peace conference, and asked them to prepare a draft of the instructions to be given to his envoy when the time came. In a very carefully worded report, the ministers, without actually saying so, managed to suggest that the main *dédommagement* should come from France, that Austria should be treated leniently, and that one must beware of Prussia and her ambitions. Specifically, they proposed the acquisition of Hildesheim, Paderborn, and some smaller territories, and an end to the alternation at Osnabruck. Correspondence on this subject continued even after George II's death in 1760. It ended only in 1762, when it became clear that Britain and France were about to conclude a separate peace, and there would be no general peace conference. The reservations already made for the quarters of the Hanoverian envoy at the proposed conference site of Augsburg were cancelled.[32]

By 1760, many people were hoping for an early end to the war. With the French driven out of Canada and India, and the Royal Navy in control of the seas, Britain's aims had been achieved. The land tax at four shillings in the pound was a heavy burden on the country squires. It was time for peace. The Prussian King was faithless and irreligious, and no true ally to the Protestant cause. The ruinous subsidy paid to him brought no advantage to England. It would do no harm to let France occupy Hanover as it could always be exchanged once Britain had gained possession of all French colonies. There were, however, others who argued that the Continental war had weakened France, made her unable to keep up her navy, and had thus left her unable to compete with English trade.[33]

Frederick was finding it more and more difficult to maintain himself against his enemies and had already asked the Knights of Malta to help him negotiate a separate peace with France, apparently without informing his British allies.[34] Late in 1760, he informed his ambassadors in London that he could not hold out forever and suggested that Britain ask the Hague to mediate a peace that would draw France out of the war. Once France had been detached from her allies, his other enemies would crumble into the dust. He adroitly changed his tune when his ambassadors reported that Britain was exhausted and longing for peace. He now declared he had no objections to a peace between Britain and France on condition that all German troops now fighting in the west be put under his command at Britain's expense.[35]

In January 1761, Mitchell was informed that Britain was prepared to make peace with France, but only out of regard for Prussia. The war overseas was burdensome, but profitable. A separate peace with France meant that Britain would forgo the part of the war advantageous to herself and be left with the dead weight of succour to the King of Prussia and the risk of exposing the Electorate to other enemies. This was the least palatable alternative in England. His Majesty was willing to save his ally, but peace with France was *only adopted as a means to save the King of Prussia* (underlined in the original). This had been constantly told to the two Prussian ambassadors in London, though in diplomatic terms. While still willing to pay subsidies to Prussia, His Majesty was not prepared to go on paying any German troops after a peace with France. As Elector, he would however permit his Hanoverian soldiers to enter Prussian service.[36]

This letter was written at a time when Pitt was still in full control of British politics, and before his successor Bute had even become Secretary for the North. It shows that there was no fundamental change in British policy towards Prussia when Bute became prime minister. Britain was ready to protect Frederick from being overwhelmed by his enemies, but would not help him to win a decisive victory over them. It does not, of course, prove that the British attitude towards peace with France was influenced by no other considerations than regard to Prussia.

Negotiations with France began in April 1761, the French chief minister having previously been told that Britain would remain faithful to her obligations as an ally of Prussia. Frederick was kept fully informed, receiving copies of all letters exchanged with France.[37] He was now anxiously hoping for an armistice between Britain and France as his military situation was becoming more and more precarious, and he barely managed to hold out till the end of the year. In September, he was informed, to his disappointment, that the peace talks had been broken off as the French conditions were totally inadmissible, both as regarded the interest and honour of His Majesty and the King of Prussia in particular.[38] It seemed likely that the Prussian army would be totally defeated in the coming year.

Frederick's hopes revived when Elizabeth of Russia, his implacable enemy, died early in 1762. She was succeeded by Peter III, a somewhat deranged young man who was a fervent admirer of the Prussian king. Peter ordered an immediate cessation of all hostilities with Prussia, and prepared to give Frederick military assistance against Austria. Frederick was already beginning to think of himself as King of Bohemia when he received disquieting news from Bute, who was by now Secretary for the North and shortly to become Prime Minister. Bute informed the Prussian ambassadors and Mitchell that the great event in the north (i.e. Elizabeth's death) had produced a change which promised an improvement in His Prussian Majesty's situation, and any aid to be furnished should only be used for the conclusion of peace. As soon as His British Majesty was satisfied on that point, the money now due under the current agreement would be sent off.[39] Frederick, confident of his friend ship with Peter, indignantly refused the offer. Bute may have had other motives for his action: his longing for peace, the growing unrest in England and the cost of a war which had just broken out with Spain, but he could not possibly have done more for Frederick. No British government could have lasted for a day once the nation discovered that its money was being used to finance the aggrandizement of one Continental state at the expense of another. If Frederick did not see this, and continued to harbour a grudge against Britain, this merely proves that he was not as much of a realist as he thought he was. He seems actually to have believed a story spread by the Russian ambassador in London that Bute was trying to incite Russia to continue the war against Prussia, a story energetically and convincingly denied by Bute.[40]

Early in June, Tsar Peter was deposed. His successor, Catherine II, put an end to friendly relations with Prussia, but did not resume the war. Prussia and Austria were now left to fight each other alone, but both countries were so exhausted that they were forced to make peace at Hubertusburg early in 1763, Frederick managing to keep Silesia. The war in the west ended with the Preliminaries of Fontainebleau in 1762, and the Peace of Paris in 1763. The French evacuated all German territories, and the British troops could return home. The Hessian and Prussian auxiliaries were disbanded, while the Hanoverian army was reduced to peacetime strength.

A *Légion Britannique* under a colonel Beckwith entered Frederick's service, where Beckwith was promoted to major-general.[41] Ferdinand of Brunswick complained bitterly about '*ce merde ministre de Bute*' and the ingratitude of which he had made his master guilty towards his allies in Germany.[42] Ferdinand had gained a reputation as one of the foremost generals of his time, a reputation he was to lose forty years later against Napoleon.

Hanover received nothing, although she had been fighting for six of the seven years of the war. Though most of the cost had been borne by Britain, the Electorate had incurred considerable debts that had not been paid back by the time of the French revolution over twenty years later. Hanover had lost many men. George II had spent his personal fortune, estimated at £2.5 million, for the defence of the Electorate. But reparations in money were practically unknown in the eighteenth century. Pitt had, indeed, once suggested that Hanover be paid £5 million, but only if she was left defenceless during the war.

During the debates in Parliament, Pitt, now out of office, thundered against Britain's abandonment of Prussia. He made much of the fact that while France had been made to promise the return of most of the territories occupied by her in Germany to the rightful owners, she was merely obliged to vacate the Prussian possessions. He overlooked the circumstance that Prussia was still at war, and giving the occupied provinces back to Prussia would have meant taking her part against Austria. When in opposition, Pitt could not always be taken seriously.

8

THE REIGN OF GEORGE III

The question whether George III was a stupid king, an evil king, or merely an honest man surrounded by incompetent advisers, is still being debated, so that it is fortunate for the student of Anglo-Hanoverian relations that he or she need not take sides in the controversy. George has always rightly been commended for never trying to influence British politics for the sake of Hanover. It is less well known that he never let British interests interfere with his Electoral affairs either.

As a youth, George disliked Hanover. This was probably due to the influence of his mother and of his father's will, both parents being decidedly against the Hanoverian connection. Young George's letter to Bute, in which he complained about the horrid Electorate 'that preys upon the very vitals of this poor kingdom' has often been printed, as has his first speech after his accession, in which he declared that: 'born and educated in this country, I glory in the name of Briton.' In 1762, two years after he had become king, he was still willing to sacrifice Hanover in order to reduce the burden of the war upon Britain. Though his subjects there would suffer immensely, he wrote to Bute, 'yet so superior is my love to this my native country over any private interests of my own . . .' that the British troops then fighting in Germany were to be ordered home.' It is, however, evident from this letter that the King was already beginning to feel some concern for his Electorate. The final change of heart must have come soon after. Throughout the rest of his reign, there is no evidence that he did not take his duties as Elector as seriously as he did those as King. George's first German testament, written in 1765, states clearly that his eldest son was to inherit Hanover according to the Imperial law of primogeniture. Although he already had a second son, there is no hint that this son should inherit the Electorate, as he might have done under George I's will.[2] Perhaps the Peace of Paris had given him leisure to become acquainted with his Electorate and the difficulties of dividing his inheritance. Possibly George had already become wearied by the intricacies of British politics and enjoyed being a ruler of a country where his orders were always obeyed.

The first Austrian ambassador to reach London after the Seven Years' War reported that he had made discreet enquiries, and had been told that George preferred both the German and French languages to English. At his introductory audience, the ambassador accordingly spoke in French, in deference to the English minister present, and noted that the minister refused to be drawn as soon as the King began to speak of Empire affairs. Of course we do not have to believe that George's knowledge of English was in any way deficient, but it is certain that he spoke German well. The Hanover archives contain a number of letters written in the King's own hand and in fluent German.[3] They include a number of mistakes in spelling and grammar, such as might have been made by any eighteenth-century German who was more used to the spoken than to the written language, but only rarely does an anglicism creep in.

If George III never visited Hanover, this was not due to a lack of interest, as is often assumed. On various occasions, he seriously thought of crossing the sea to visit his dynasty's homeland. Thus he informed his Hanoverian ministers in 1770 that he was planning a visit in the near future.[4] In 1781, he had two coaches made in England and sent to Hanover to be reserved 'until our arrival'.[5] A few years later, he ordered repairs to the palace at Hanover to be postponed 'until we have inspected the building ourselves',[6] and in 1789 he wrote to his son Prince Augustus that he should not be surprised if he were called to Hanover and

Richmond d. 29t. Oct. 1771.

Meine geheimten, Rath und Cammer Præsident. Die berichte welche bey dem Courier überhabracht geworden laeten mir sehr kümmerlich; der Zustand meiner getroffenen ist jämmerlich. Ich hoffe die Cammer hat doch ihrigen gethan werden fernlen konnte zu fullen so die fluten zugeschworen worden. Ich habe beym Courier befohlen der Kuren soll bey der Cammer vorgenandert wagen dauslaen oder ich beständig weil daß Lmingrs greßölben und din Naton Soßben zu gelten weil fallaen din nurzigen resourcen in unehaunen fällen, und darum müßen nicht ausgenomrüst zu sein. Ich habe schon befohlen daß das vorräthigen geld in Akea bringe one die Cammer zu 3. pr. cent verzinset werden soll.

F.

Windsor d 24ten Junÿ 178.

Meine Feldt Marschall[...] Sohn dem Hauptmann wird
[...] dessen Dienst [...]; [...] conduite in England
[...] völlig mein beyfal[...] ein [...] ihm [...]
in den neuen Battaillons zu dienen [...]
Companie zu hülfe zu kommen. Ich meine daß das Hauptmann
[...] die [...] fordern [...] in die leichte Dragoner
gesetzet zu [...] Esländer im Lande zu kommen
[...] meinen Sohn hoffe ich [...] bald nach Göttingen
gehen, ein gute anziehung ist allen Officier [...]
und ich schmeichle mich daß dieser [...] sehr [...]
junge [...] wird mit der zeit [...]
dienst [...].

George R

found his father and the Queen there.[7] These plans were real, and had nothing to do with George's occasional threats to abdicate and retire to Hanover. The reason that the King never actually undertook any of these contemplated journeys was simply that he did not like travelling. Even at home, he never got as far as the north of England, let alone Wales, Scotland, or Ireland.

In 1764, George appointed his second son Frederick, later Duke of York, Bishop of Osnabruck at the tender age of one. As they grew older, all his sons, with the exception of the Prince of Wales, were sent to Hanover in order to learn German as well as to escape the influence of their elder brother and lead a more moral life than he. (Both objects were only partially achieved.) Gradually, the King's involvement with Hanoverian affairs increased. He became so wrapped up in Electoral matters that in 1785 Charles James Fox, who had been Britain's first Foreign Secretary only a few years before, told the Russian ambassador that George's main political concern was with Hanover.[8] The King took a personal interest in many details of the administration. He ordered the country to be surveyed and maps to be prepared. The construction of the first paved long-distance roads in the Electorate was largely due to the royal initiative. Under his direction, efforts were made to further what little industry there was, especially the processing of agricultural products such as wood and flax. The King did not hesitate to antagonize the guilds which kept the linen industry bound by antiquated regulations and prevented it from competing effectively with imports, even though his reforms tended to reduce English exports to Hanover. Special tax reductions were made in order to introduce new manufactures, such as the production of fayence, mirrors, and lace, the King asking for samples to be sent to London for his inspection. He even approved of the payment of a sum of money to the Hanoverian minister in London that was to enable him to discover the secret of manufacturing a type of linen that was both white and shiny, whether legitimately or through industrial espionage, we are not told.[9] Only George's personal insistence brought about the release of the peasants on the Electoral domains from the corvée, though the owners of private estates did not follow his example, as he had hoped. The King's main interest, however, apart from the promotion of agriculture, to be described in the following chapter, was the furthering of education. He continued a programme begun by his grandfather (George II) for giving public assistance to communities wishing to build schools, and supplemented the salary of the most needy schoolmasters. The university of Gottingen was enabled to award five annual prizes to the best students, and money was provided to buy books for its library.[10]

For Hanover, as for other Continental states, the years after the peace of 1763 were a time of peaceful recovery after the war. The people missed their monarch. Though the King's brothers, the Dukes of York and Gloucester, paid visits in 1765 and 1769, this was felt to be a poor substitute for the actual presence of the sovereign. When the Prince of Wurttemberg, the King's son-in-law, travelled through the country in 1797, the peasants in all the places he passed through entreated him to persuade His Majesty to come among them.[11] The King did not appear, and they had to content themselves with the reflection that God also was invisible, but they still knew he was there.

Maria Theresa's husband Francis died in 1765, and his son Joseph became Emperor. Though all real power remained in the hands of his mother as Queen of Bohemia and Hungary, Joseph was still able to exert some influence on the internal affairs of the Empire, where he wished to strengthen the central authority. It was probably due to Joseph's policy that in 1774 the Austrian ambassador complained to the court in London about the conduct of the Hanoverian ministry, accusing it of using a rude and insolent tone in its communications with Vienna, quite different from that employed by His Majesty's British ministers. The ambassador, Belgioioso, first approached the Hanoverian minister in London, but received only a vague answer. He then addressed his complaint to the Earl of Suffolk, Secretary of State for the North. Suffolk told him that while the King was known to be devoted to Austria, his British ministers, including himself, knew little about the Empire, and would never interfere in Electoral affairs. Suffolk promised that he would speak to the King about the matter, but did not dare to keep his word. Lord North, the Prime Minister, also thought it was impossible to do anything in the matter. He told the ambassador that he was happy to know that relations between the Emperor and His Majesty were good, but the attitude of the Hanoverian ministry was not his concern. When Belgioioso approached Lord Rochford, who had succeeded Suffolk, his reception was slightly more favourable. According to Rochford, Britain was always interested in Empire affairs, but it was difficult for ministers to talk to the King about such matters except at the royal initiative. Rochford nevertheless spoke to the King, but must have received a reprimand, for he now told the ambassador that he was convinced that the fault lay with the Imperial court. Furthermore, Hanoverian affairs were none of his business, and he ought not even have talked to Belgioioso about them. The ambassador's conclusion was that George did not see, and did not want to see, Hanoverian matters except through the eyes of his Electoral ministers.[12] It seems that the Emperor's complaint was dropped after George had threatened to withdraw his envoy from Vienna, and ministers had begun to adopt a more polite tone.[13]

☆ ☆ ☆

The unrest that had broken out in the American colonies did not affect Germany. When war began in 1775, the British government, as in 1715 and 1745, refrained from using Hanoverian soldiers to fight the rebels, as this would have increased the colonists' resentment against the King. Troops from other German states, such as Hesse and Brunswick, were hired instead. The ministers did, however, ask for 12000 men from the Electorate to garrison Gibraltar and Minorca in order to free British soldiers for service across the ocean. George agreed to this request and gave orders for the soldiers to be sent, leaving his Hanoverian ministers only four weeks' time for the preparations. The troops were taken directly to their destination without landing in England.

The news that foreign soldiers were being used to guard British possessions aroused great indignation in Parliament.[14]

Many of the independent country gentlemen rebelled. They claimed that it was illegal and unconstitutional for the Crown to introduce foreigners into British dominions without the consent of Parliament. It was suggested that the deployment of the Hanoverian troops was due to the 'overriding influence' of the King. The Prime Minister, Lord North, in vain declared that he had advised the measure himself. The Commons were not satisfied until he promised to bring the question before the House. The reaction in the House of Lords was similar. There it was pointed out that the employment of Hanoverian troops on British territory was dangerous to the constitution and the country because they were not subject to British military law. During the ensuing debate the Commons left the question open and undecided,[15] while the Lords voted by 75 to 32 that the bringing of foreign troops into British territory without previous consent of Parliament was dangerous and unconstitutional. The Commons thereupon passed a bill of indemnity, freeing ministers from responsibility, but this was thrown out by the Lords on the grounds that the bill was self-contradictory because its preamble stated that no offence had been committed. If this were true, there was no need to exonerate the ministers. Furthermore, passing the bill would imply approval of the stationing of foreign troops in British possessions. There the matter rested.

The reason why Parliament could not or would not make up its mind on the question of the Hanoverian soldiers in the Mediterranean was probably that their presence there was felt to be necessary, while the principle that soldiers from another country could be stationed in British dominions at ministers' discretion was inadmissible. The government was content with this indecisive outcome, and the Hanoverians stayed on. They fought well, and helped defend Gibraltar successfully against the Spanish. Minorca, however was lost, and the Hanoverians were returned to Britain on Spanish ships. None reached home before 1784.

The forces sent to Gibraltar and Minorca were simply part of the regular army detached for special service at short notice. A much more careful method of selection was used when the King acceded to the East India Company's request for a contingent to serve in Asia. Ministers were ordered to ask for volunteers from the officers and cadets of the infantry and cavalry to make up the nucleus of the battalions to be formed, while the ranks were to be filled with foreigners willing to serve abroad for eight years. Care was to be taken not to infringe the laws of the Empire and to avoid detrimental effects on the Electorate's own forces. Four thousand men were duly found and sent to India, where they took part, for example, in the battle of Cuddalore.[16]

Trouble on the Continent began in 1777, when the Wittelsbach line reigning in Bavaria died out and the succession fell to a distant agnate. Maria Theresa wanted to use this opportunity to revive an old plan of the Habsburgs, and exchange the distant and troublesome Austrian Netherlands for a more convenient territory adjacent to her hereditary states. The acquisition of Bavaria would have given the House of Austria a dominant and unassailable position in southern Germany, and possibly a base for reuniting the Empire under Habsburg rule. This prospect was intolerable to Frederick II of Prussia, and he declared war, knowing that both Britain and France were occupied elsewhere. There was not much fighting in this conflict, called the War of the Bavarian Succession in eighteenth-century fashion, but nicknamed the 'potato war' by the irreverent (the Prussians spent much of their time digging potatoes), because Catherine of Russia intervened. She threatened both parties and forced them to accept Russo-French mediation. Maria Theresa had to give up the proposed exchange and content herself with a slice of Bavaria on her side of the river Inn, unknowingly ensuring that one day Adolf Hitler would be born an Austrian.

When the new line on the Bavarian throne was also about to die out a few years later, and the succession was due to fall to another distant agnate, Joseph II, now Maria Theresa's heir, made another attempt to exchange the Netherlands for Bavaria. He had prepared his ground better than his mother. Through concessions in the Balkans, he had obtained an alliance with Catherine and her consent to the proposed transaction. Joseph was also allied with France, so that Prussia stood alone against both Austria and Russia. Her only potential ally among the great powers, Britain, was exhausted after fighting the Americans and the French, and not particularly interested in Continental affairs. Frederick II, resourceful as ever, solved the problem by forming a league of Princes (*Furstenbund*) to 'defend the ancient rights of the Empire'. The first states to join Prussia were Hanover and Saxony, who were soon followed by most of the smaller principalities in central Germany and some in the south. The *Furstenbund* grew quickly because the partner states were afraid of Joseph's ambitions. At the time, he was seeking to extend the influence of the Imperial power, and — so it was feared — re-establish Catholic ascendancy by installing members of his family in the ecclesiastical territories of the north, including Hildesheim and Paderborn, both long coveted by Hanover. George III joined the *Furstenbund* as Elector without consulting his British ministers. When the Russian ambassador spoke of the matter to Pitt (the younger Pitt, recently appointed Prime Minister), the minister had to write to the King in order to know what answer to give, being careful to avoid offence by adding that it was not within the province of His Majesty's servants to give an opinion on the matter. He was told that the King's conduct had been actuated by his duty to the stability of the Empire, and that the Russians had no right to interfere.[17]

The *Furstenbund* proved too strong for Joseph to overcome its resistance, but he did not resign easily. Austria had already declared that she had given up the idea of an exchange as soon as she had been notified that the new heir to Bavaria was opposed to it. Nevertheless, throughout the summer of 1785, the Austrian and Russian ambassadors to London, with the Russian taking the lead, tried to persuade the British ministers that they should prevent Hanover from joining the *Furstenbund*, or at least delay ratification of her accession. The official answer to their representations was that Britain could not interfere with Hanover because it was an independent country, and that in any event, there was no reason for interference because the *Furstenbund* was only intended to maintain the status quo. Less officially, the ambassadors were told that the King always grew very angry when approached by his British ministers about Hanoverian affairs, that he disliked the King of Prussia intensely, but would not change his mind once it was made up, and that the King's royal dignity would suffer if he were forced to depart from the course he had chosen. For the ministry to put pressure on the King was unthinkable unless he received adequate compensation, such as an alliance with the two Imperial powers, an alliance which could only be contemplated if they directly or indirectly broke their friendship with the Bourbons in France and Spain.

The two ambassadors did not know what to make of this. They explained in vain that two countries under the same monarch must necessarily have the same foreign policy, especially, in this case, in Germany. If Britain desired an alliance with Austria and Russia, how could the King as Elector conclude an alliance with their enemy Prussia? In their reports to Vienna and St. Petersburg, they gave various reasons for their lack of success: the King told his ministers nothing about his affairs in Germany; the ministers were ill-informed and repeated only what they heard from Hanover; the government was too weak to oppose the King's wishes; the whole thing was a plot to bring about an alliance with Austria and Russia against France. In their frustration, the Russians even threatened Britain with the Tsarina's formal displeasure if Hanover were to join the *Furstenbund*, perhaps in the hope of stirring up the opposition in Parliament as well as alarming the merchants trading with Russia, whose business was very profitable.[18]

The British government remained unperturbed. As the Foreign Secretary, Lord Carmarthen, wrote to the British ambassador to St Petersburg, who had been subjected to the same pressure, Russia's threat of an alliance with France was irreconcilable with her declaration that France was in league with Prussia, Russia's enemy. Russia also had a quarrel with France because she wished to expand her territory in the Balkans at the expense of Turkey, a design which was opposed by the French. The prospect of a Franco-Russian alliance could therefore be discounted, though developments must be closely watched.[19] Hanover and Great Britain had the same sovereign and were bound by a natural and permanent connection. It was very improbable that the interests of the two countries in foreign affairs should be totally inconsistent with each other. Though under such circumstances it was obvious that Britain must take the lead, it by no means followed that a measure of internal precaution confined to Germany should be binding on the British government.[20] Carmarthen did not mention what may have been another reason for British reluctance to interfere. An independent Belgium under a Wittelsbach prince might easily come under French influence, and one of the main objects of British policy was to keep the French out of the Low Countries.

Frederick, on his part, tried to gain British friendship by throwing out broad hints that he would like an Anglo-Prussian alliance. He pointed out that the balance of power in Europe had changed, and that the two countries were now isolated. He rediscovered his attachment to Britain, and declared his earnest wish to cultivate the closest intimacy with His Majesty both as King and as Elector. The British government did not respond to these overtures. Carmarthen distrusted Prussia, whom he believed to be still too closely connected with France. Only if the Emperor and France were to form some plan of aggrandizement (i.e. attack Prussia) could a closer connection be considered.[21]

The question of Hanover's participation in the *Furstenbund* was brought before Parliament on 24 and 25 January 1786 during the debate on the King's speech. Charles James Fox, speaking for the opposition, asserted that the League had caused dissension between Britain and Austria, and thus helped France by weakening the Emperor. He ridiculed the distinction between the King and the Elector, asking whether British troops would one day have to fight against a Hanoverian army led by the Elector? Pitt replied that the merits and demerits of the Germanic confederacy were of no concern to His Majesty's ministers, that chance had placed the sovereignty of the two countries in the same hands, but it by no means followed that their interests must always be the same, though it might be to their mutual advantage to make them reconcilable. Britain was in no way bound by the Elector's policies. If British ministers were made responsible for the government of Hanover, the Electorate would become a limb and member of the British Empire and be entitled to demand its protection.[22]

Frederick II died in August 1786, and his successor gradually lost interest in the *Furstenbund*. Its main aim, to prevent the exchange of Bavaria and the Austrian Netherlands, had been achieved. By 1788, Prussia had managed to enter into an alliance with the maritime powers, i.e. Britain and the Netherlands, and felt secure against Habsburg aggression. Hanover now tried to use the *Furstenbund* for the purpose of building up a clientele of lesser states in Germany and in this way to establish a power base that might enable the Electorate to face Prussia on equal terms. Some progress was made in this direction, and it is not impossible that Hanover might have achieved its aim of forming a third force within the Empire if this policy had been carried out more energetically, but this would have required a greater statesman than Hanover possessed, or could be expected to possess, at the time. The *Furstenbund* began to decline because of internal rivalries, and was practically dead before it was forgotten during the wars following the French revolution.[23]

The episode of the *Furstenbund* is interesting because it shows how complicated British-Hanoverian relations could become. Hanover concluded an alliance with Prussia in 1785 without consulting the British government, although at the time Britain considered Prussia a client state of her enemy France. A few years later, when Prussia had become Britain's ally, the Electorate pursued a policy contrary to Prussian interests. Yet little Hanover would never have dared to displease mighty Prussia if she had not had the backing of Britain through the Personal Union. True, Britain was not obliged to defend Hanover in purely German quarrels, but no Prussian minister would care to find out whether she would really remain a disinterested spectator in a serious conflict.

George had suffered a first nervous breakdown in 1765, and during the following years his mental condition had repeatedly given cause for anxiety. Around the beginning of the 1790s, this old tendency to insanity reasserted itself. He became more and more feeble-minded and was frequently unable to attend to business properly. It is often impossible to tell whether statements attributed to him during his later years were his own or were issued by his ministers in his name. His eyesight began to fail, and the rule that all letters to Hanover must be signed by the King had to be relaxed, the Hanoverian minister now signing correspondence on his own responsibility. But as long as George retained some of his faculties, he did not forget his Electorate. We read that in 1805 'the little energy of the King's mind looks to Hanover'.[24] At last, in 1810, he was declared unfit to reign, and the Prince of Wales was appointed Prince Regent. The King died in 1820, succeeded by his son as George IV.

9

CULTURAL AND TRADE RELATIONS

During the eighteenth century, Britain rose to pre-eminence in almost every field of human endeavour, the main exception being music. British political institutions, philosophy, science, literature, economics, agriculture, and engineering were admired and envied by all Europe. Men such as Hume, Newton, Adam Smith, Arthur Young, Capability Brown, Reynolds, Fielding, and Cook were known to every educated person in the western world. It was impossible for a small territory like Hanover to remain unaffected by this pervasive British influence. The concern of this study is to determine how much of this influence was due to the Personal Union, and whether things might have developed differently without it.

The University of Gottingen was founded in 1734, during the reign of George II, and still bears his name. Though of course his approval was necessary, and readily obtained, he had little to do with the institution. The real founder was the chief minister G. Adolf von Munchhausen, who was motivated by quarrels with Brunswick-Wolfenbuttel over the university at Helmstedt, until then jointly supported by the Guelf states. Instead of using Oxford or Cambridge as the model for his new academy, Munchhausen preferred to follow the pattern of the renowned university of Halle, his own Alma Mater. The languages used at Gottingen were German, Latin, and French, and a John Thompson taught English there as early as 1735.

As the university grew, interest in England and the English language increased. Books and instruments were ordered from London, and many professors travelled to England, putting their experiences to use in their writings, in which they praised the English constitution, the absence of class distinctions, and the liberty of the press.[1] The most famous of these was the philosopher G.C. Lichtenberg, who later became the teacher of George II's sons. Many English books were translated at Gottingen, among them Adam Smith's *Wealth of Nations* which appeared there in the same year it was published in England. Young Englishmen often came to study at Gottingen, the most prominent being Samuel Taylor Coleridge, Thomas Young the naturalist, and the three younger sons of George III. The links forged between Gottingen and Britain during these early years have endured, and Gottingen is still a chief centre of anglistic studies in Germany.

Other cultural contacts probably included many visits of Hanoverians to England. All Electoral subjects were allowed to travel to London to lay personal petitions before the King, and the practice seems to have become so frequent that special regulations had to be issued prohibiting people from begging for money to pay their travelling expenses. It was further forbidden to approach the King in a matter pending before a court of law.[2] Unfortunately, there are no sources that would enable us to estimate the number of travellers with anything like accuracy. Many people are known to have visited England only from a note in their biographies, and it is likely that London was included in the grand tour of most young Hanoverian nobles. A number of students received grants to study in England. Sometimes they did not want to return home,[3] a problem not unknown in modern times. It is also known that in 1770 a delegation of Harz miners rendered homage to George III at Kew, and that he showed them the Prince of Wales as their future sovereign.[4] It is likely that there were many such visits. Occasionally, one comes across bits of tantalizing information, for instance that one of Burke's friends was a Hanoverian and that a Hanoverian took part in at least one of Cook's voyages.[5] Surely both these cases were somehow connected with the Personal Union, but more details are not available. In 1820, there were over twenty Hanoverian consulates in Britain, more than half of those the country maintained abroad, but it cannot be concluded that their number was justified by the traffic between the two countries. Nearly all consuls bore English names, and we may presume that these appointments were more a way of honouring old comrades-in-arms from the Napoleonic wars than the result of the need to look after Hanoverian visitors.[6]

Perhaps the most valuable acquisition Britain gained from Hanover was William Herschel, who as a young man fled to England in 1757 to escape the invading French. Having taught himself astronomy, he became one of the great astronomers of all times, among other things discovering the planet Uranus, which he loyally named 'Georgium Sidus' after George III. Thoroughly anglicized, he was granted a knighthood for his work. While his sister Caroline, who had helped him and might have shared his fame in an age less prejudiced against women, returned to Hanover after his death, his son remained to become a famous astronomer in his turn. English literature owes a minor debt to the Personal Union in the *Adventures of Baron Munchhausen*, written in English in 1785 by R.E. Raspe, and only later translated into German. Munchhausen is known as a historical personage who lived in the Electorate and was evidently a good storyteller. Two Hanoverian artists, G. Wessel, a sculptor from Osnabruck, and J.H. Ramberg, a painter, are known to have spent many years in England and to have been much influenced by what they learnt there. But Hanoverians in general were not inclined to follow British leadership in the arts blindly. When some of Turner's pictures were exhibited at Hanover in 1836, the public turned away from these 'wild daubs'.[7]

Not all visitors from Hanover were overawed by what they found in England. A certain Beckmann travelling to

Manchester to see the Duke of Bridgewater's famous canal rather patronizingly remarked that the time for navigable canals had now arrived in England also. He admired the looms of Manchester, but thought that a better mechanic could improve them so as to require fewer workmen. It was, however, according to Beckmann, important to keep people in employment, and this was also the reason why there were no sawmills in England.[8] Beckmann later wrote a book on agronomy which ignored British advances on the subject.

As the years progressed, the young bloods of the city of Hanover, the students of Gottingen, and even some of the professors took to aping English dress and English manners, much to the disgust of the more sober members of the population. This proved to be a transient fashion which disappeared with the Personal Union without ever having touched the people in general.[9]

Concerning trade relations, neither the British nor the Hanoverian government ever made an attempt to coordinate the economic policies of the two countries, and both sides kept their customs barriers. There were, however, a number of attempts by private persons to exploit the connnection between the kingdom and the Electorate commercially. As early as 1709, an 'English Manufacturing Company' was founded at the small port of Harburg (now a part of Hamburg). Half of the members of the governing board were British, while the other half were appointed by the Hanoverian government. By 1719, the company, evidently having failed to make a profit, applied for permission to extend its operations to the production of soap, as well as dried and salted fish, and asked for customs protection against rivals.[10] The venture never seems to have attained any importance, though there were still twenty-seven British nationals living at Harburg in 1720. Suggestions to develop the port of Harburg continued to be made throughout the eighteenth century. In 1728, George II, continuing a project initiated by his father, supported a plan to widen the approach channel and turn Harburg into the staple for British goods, but the Hanoverian government thought the idea both hopeless and dangerous.[11] Two or three years later a venture to establish Harburg as a base for a herring fleet failed because of lack of interest both locally and at government level.[12] Five different attempts to found a Hanoverian East India Company — to be affiliated to the London East India Company — were made between 1720 and 1750. Such a plan might have met with some success because the Hanoverian company could perhaps have helped the British to overcome Dutch competition on the German market. Although the entire capital was to be provided from private sources, the project foundered on the opposition of the Hanoverian ministry, which alleged that the activities of the company would lead to an excess of imports that Hanover, with its small volume of exports, could not pay for.[13]

The reluctance of the ministry to enter into these various schemes was doubtless partly due to the ministers' innate conservatism, but there were other arguments as well. The independent port cities of Hamburg and Bremen already provided a satisfactory service for their hinterland. The proposed ventures would have met with stiff and experienced competition. Even if successful, they might have brought more disadvantages than benefits to Hanover, for they could have weakened the city of Hamburg, which was needed as a strong bulwark against Denmark.

When the Electorate sent out two whaling ships, they met with a friendly reception from their British colleagues, perhaps because the Hanover flag, altered by George I in 1714, was very similar to the British.[14] There must have been more Hanoverian merchantmen on the high seas about which there seems to be no record. When, in 1760, Britain concluded a treaty of peace and commerce with Morocco, an article was included according to which Hanoverian ships were to be given the same treatment as British vessels. A similar provision was inserted into the 1816 treaties with Algiers, Tunis, and Tripoli, making the Hanover flag much sought after by German merchants from other states.

☆   ☆   ☆

During the early years of the Personal Union, there is no

evidence of British influence on agriculture in Hanover. Potatoes began to be grown there in 1720, but the crop seems to have been introduced from France or the Low Countries rather than from England. On George II's orders, turnips were planted in 1748, but their cultivation met with no success. Hanoverian farmers continued to grow corn (chiefly rye), which was their main crop, vegetables, and various plants furnishing raw materials such as flax and timber. Pastures and cattle-breeding were relatively neglected.[15]

On instructions signed by George II, and possibly at his personal initiative, a stud farm was founded at Celle in 1735. Its first manager was an Englishman, Gabriel Roger Brown, who soon built up a flourishing business, not only providing horses for Hanoverian agriculture, but also exporting foals and cavalry remounts to neighbouring countries. The breed was improved by a gift of twenty-six English thoroughbred stallions from the Duke of Cumberland shortly before he became King of Hanover, and Hanoverian horses have been held in high regard ever since.

Under George III, government activity in agriculture increased. George was an enthusiastic farmer — in England he was nicknamed 'Farmer George' — and made many efforts to improve farming practices in his Electorate. He is perhaps best remembered in Hanover for the foundation of an agricultural society (*Königlich-Grossbritamische und Churfürstlich-Braunschweig-Lüneburgsche Landwirtschaftsgesellschaft*). This society is said to have been started on his initiative and to have been the instrument for the dissemination of English agricultural methods and machinery in the Electorate and beyond. Alas, recent research has shown that this fame is not deserved.[16] The idea of founding the society did not stem from George, but from one of the chief minister's relatives, Otto von Munchhausen, and a group of associates, only one of whom (von Hinuber) is known to have visited England, and only during his grand tour some twenty years earlier. The society was indeed constituted on the model of the 'London Society for the Encouragement of Arts, Manufactures, and Commerce', but this was hardly extraordinary. The English society was the first of its kind, and had already served as the prototype for similar societies in other parts of Germany, as well as in France and Switzerland. Of course the sovereign's consent had to be obtained, and was graciously granted, but the praise given to George as the enlightened founder was no more than the lip service expected according to the spirit of the times. Besides, this form of adulation brought the society a number of privileges and generous financial support. Nor did the society look primarily to England for the pattern of its activities. It did indeed propagate the new idea of the rotation of crops, but preferred the inferior North German system to the better English one. Cattle were bought in Frisia and Jutland, and sheep in Spain, ignoring the superior English breeds. When chance put the society into possession of some English agricultural machinery (see below), the machines were kept in store for many years before at last copies were made and sold in the Electorate and neighbouring countries.[17]

The attitude of the society — favouring by now outdated German methods and machinery — did not change until the 1790s, when A.D. Thaer, a native of Celle, rose to a prominent position in its management. Thaer has been called the pioneer of agronomy in Germany, and is still remembered. His first important book was an *Introduction to the knowledge of English agriculture*, and he continued his interest in the more advanced system of agronomy developed in England throughout his life. Under Thaer's influence, the Hanover society began to actively propagate English agricultural methods, to build English-style machinery for sale both at home and abroad, copying those already in its possession. It continued to do so after he had left the country to take service in Prussia. Unfortunately, there is nothing to show that Thaer's career had anything to do with the Personal Union. It is quite likely that he would have reached the same conclusions about the more advanced state of English agriculture, and would have spread his knowledge in the same manner, if he had been born in some German state not linked with Britain.

An example of Hanoverian lack of interest in British developments is the case of C. Bruggmann (or Brüggemann). Long after other German states, especially Prussia, had learnt to profit from English advances in agronomy,

Bruggmann, a young peasant, was sent to England in 1778, at George III's suggestion.[18] There he was to learn modern methods of cultivating heathland, which covered large parts of the Electorate. After three years in England, Bruggmann returned to Hanover, where he refused to take up the land allotted to him, and demanded that he be given better soil to work on. This request was denied, and Bruggmann went back to England, where he seems to have been quite successful. Perhaps Bruggmann is not altogether to be blamed, for he had not been trained on poor land, but at Petersham and Esher, where his teacher was the well-known agronomist Duckett. But nobody seems to have thought of putting a little pressure on Bruggmann to demonstrate what skills he had acquired, or of sending someone else to England to learn the techniques Hanover needed. On his return to England, Bruggmann left behind the agricultural machines he had brought with him, and they were handed to the agricultural society. Their subsequent fate has already been described.

One of George III's pet projects for Hanover was the enclosure of common land. There can be no doubt that his enthusiasm for this came from his knowledge of conditions in England. There, this was the age of the great enclosure acts, the beneficial effects of which were praised by everybody except the very poor who lost their livelihood for a sum of money they could do little with.

Considerable progress in enclosures had already been made in the duchy of Lauenburg, which however was not part of the ancient Guelf states, and where the structure of agriculture was quite different from that of the rest of the Electorate. George heard of these reforms shortly after he became king, and in 1765 told the ministry to promote enclosures in other parts of the country, beginning with the duchy of Luneburg. By 1768, the ministry had prepared a royal edict which treated not only of enclosures, but also of other agricultural matters, having, as it turned out, no visible effect on the former. On 16 February 1779, the King at last issued a formal order to the ministry to press forward with enclosures as quickly as possible, and to report on the success of the measures taken.[19] From then on until 1796, the ministers reported once a year on the progress achieved (very little), and the King as regularly replied that he approved of their measures and hoped for more speed. It was not until June 1802 that a law on enclosures was finally enacted, possibly under Thaer's influence. The effects of this law, the first of its kind in Germany, were beneficial, and much hitherto uncultivated land came under the plough. Hanover even had to call in settlers from other parts of Germany to make full use of the new opportunities. Almost forty years had been lost.

As in agriculture, Hanover was slow to imitate the technical progress achieved by Britain in the Industrial Revolution. As late as 1806, the owner of a paper mill who wished to introduce a steam engine to modernize his plant was forbidden to do so by the ministry.[20] Where the use of machinery for industrial purposes was permitted, it was imported from England and had to be returned there if repairs became necessary. It was not until 1834 that a local factory began to build machines of its own. The introduction of street lighting met with better success. In 1824, a British company began to build a gas works and to supply gas for the street lamps of the city of Hanover, the utility remaining in British ownership for nearly a hundred years. A polytechnic was opened in 1831, but as the founders wished to reduce British influence rather than increase it, they preferred to copy the polytechnics of Berlin and Vienna rather than British ones. Attempts to build a railway in Hanover after the first trains had begun to run in England were frustrated by the Duke of Cumberland, and public sentiment agreed with him in spite of pressure from the Duke of Brunswick. Not until 1843, long after the end of the Personal Union, were British engineers called in to build a railway line.

It is evident that Hanover did not take full advantage of the intellectual and commercial opportunities open to the Electorate by its association with Britain. It is not impossible that Hanover could have become the leader of Germany in the fields of agriculture, industry, and democratic politics if she had determinedly followed the British example. But the inhabitants of Lower Saxony have always been noted for calm imperturbability rather than for volatile lusting after change. (One author calls them intelligent, but not intellectual.)[21] This traditionalist attitude was especially evident when the country was governed by an exclusive nobility, essentially complacent and resistant to change, and without the presence of a monarch willing and able to enforce progress, as was the case in some other German states, notably Prussia. Doubtless there was also conscious or unconscious resistance against the influence of Hanover's powerful associate. Fearful of losing their identity and becoming an inferior sort of Englishman, Hanoverians preferred to retain their traditions and depend on their own resources. Unlike most German states, where the Anglophiles were in the majority, the Anglophobes prevailed in Hanover.[22] It must be remembered that Hanover was a poor, almost exclusively agrarian country, the Harz mines having become exhausted in the course of the century. There was little free capital, and the danger of the country's being overwhelmed by foreign entrepreneurs was somewhat more than imaginary.

10

THE NAPOLEONIC AGE

The news of the revolutionary events in France was at first received with enthusiasm by many Germans, especially the upper middle class. The abolition of the privileges of the nobles, the freeing of the serfs, and the restriction of the king's powers by means of a constitution, all seemed to herald an epoch of advancement for all humankind. Meetings were held to celebrate the new era in several cities and at some universities, including that of Gottingen. As the excesses of the revolutionaries became known, and especially after the execution of Louis XVI, all but a small minority turned away from the radical teachings of Paris. Foremost among the opponents of revolutionary ideas were two Hanoverians, Brandes and Rehberg. Brandes, the friend of Burke mentioned in the previous chapter, and his associate Rehberg, set forth Burke's doctrine that all progress must be gradual and tempered with due regard for existing rights and traditions. Burke's *Reflections on the Revolution in France* had already been translated by one of Kant's pupils.[1]

The personal danger to which the French king was subjected by the revolutionaries had brought about a form of understanding between those ancient rivals, Austria and Prussia, even before his end on the scaffold. Though neither wished to interfere in France, both monarchs felt they must protect their own thrones.[2] When the French government declared war against Austria in 1792, Prussia therefore came to her aid. The ensuing war went badly for the allies.

They were overconfident, and their commander, Ferdinand of Brunswick, had lost the youthful decisiveness he had shown during the Seven Years' War. Besides, both Austria and Prussia had to keep a watchful eye on Catherine of Russia. Two thousand miles away from Paris, Catherine was ready enough to denounce the revolutionaries, but more interested in expanding her western frontiers than in the French form of government. At the end of the year, the French had occupied Mainz (Mayence), Aachen (Aix-la-Chapelle), and Brussels.

The occupation of German terrritory by the French caused the Empire to declare war, and Britain followed shortly afterwards because of the danger to the Netherlands, so that Hanover was now a belligerent. The Electorate sent 12000 men to join the British army in Flanders, while it preferred to fulfil its obligations to the Empire by the payment of a sum of money. The campaigns of 1793 and 1794, after initial successes, again ended in disaster, with the French in possession of the entire left bank of the Rhine, including Holland. Prussia now withdrew from the war against the revolutionaries. She was more interested in the division of Poland than in the defence of her western territories, and had only been kept in the alliance during 1794 by lavish subsidies from Britain and Holland. In April 1795, the King of Prussia, wishing to use all his troops for the conquest of Warsaw, concluded the peace of Basel (Bâle) with France. He agreed to cede all his rights and territories on the left bank of the Rhine against a French promise to respect the neutrality of northern Germany east of a demarcation line which left Hanover and Westfalia on the Prussian side. This treacherous desertion earned Prussia the hatred and contempt of her allies, even though the other powers could hardly be accused of unselfish devotion to the common cause.[3]

During the fighting in Flanders, the Hanoverians had so distinguished themselves that the Duke of Cumberland, one of George III's sons, wrote to the King on one occasion that 'nothing but their amazing bravery . . . has saved us'. By the end of 1794, the Anglo-Hanoverian army had been driven back across the river Ems, and the Electorate was threatened by a French invasion. The King hoped that the

British would help him to defend the land of his ancestors and complained to Pitt in March 1795 that the French were willing to treat with all Germany except the Electorate because it belonged to him. This gave him a 'fair right' to call upon England to cover Hanover. 'I own I feel for my subjects on this occasion', he wrote.[4] When he heard of the peace of Basel, he found it 'unwise as well as highly blamable'.[5] His Electoral ministers were eager for the country to be included in the Basel neutrality zone, but the King could not make up his mind. Although there were British troops stationed in the Electorate, he continued to procrastinate without informing his British ministers of his actions. On 13 July, Pitt had to ask him for some explanation of the Hanover ministry's hesitant conduct, because otherwise the exertion and expense of maintaining British troops in that country would be unavailing.[6] Finally on 25 August, the last day on which he could have done so, George declared that he would not oppose neutrality. His Majesty's British servants, who had hoped he would opt for active resistance against France, resignedly decided they must do the best they could.[7] Under Prussian pressure, the British troops and the French émigrés still in Hanover had to leave.[8] Maintaining neutrality proved to be a heavy burden on the Electorate because it had to pay large sums for the upkeep of the Prussian soldiers who were now stationed in the country. To make matters worse, the Prussians did not even defend the demarcation line energetically. George had hardly agreed to its establishment when a French army crossed the Rhine because it happened to suit their convenience. The French remained on the Prussian side of the line until driven back by the Austrians.

After Basel, fighting continued in southern Germany and Italy, with fortune sometimes favouring one side, and sometimes the other, until a young French general, Napoleon Bonaparte, forced the Austrians to agree to the peace of Campoformio (1 August 1797), the Austrians giving up all claims on the left bank of the Rhine. The treaty contained an article promising the deposed Stadtholder of the Netherlands compensation for his loss by giving him a suitable territory in Germany. Where this was to be was left unspecified, though during the preliminary negotiations the French had demanded that he be given Hanover.[9] Further details were to be settled by a general peace congress to be held at Rastatt. The negotiations continued for nearly two years without leading to any conclusion, partly because the French continued in their aggressiveness, and partly because of the attitude of the other great powers. Britain and France could not come to any agreement, while Tsar Paul of Russia, Catherine's successor, was angered when Napoleon, on his expedition to Egypt, occupied the island of Malta, which was under his protection. Austria now felt inclined to try the fortunes of war once more, and naturally wished to have the Empire on her side. Several states opposed Austria's policy, among them Hanover, and the Austrians angrily complained to the British ambassador, Lord Minto, who reported to London. Lord Grenville, the Foreign Secretary, wrote to Minto that he had informed the King. Though it was perhaps not for him (Grenville) to give an opinion, he did not think that Hanover should give up the protection of Prussia in the expectation of receiving help from Austria. This was to be lamented, but no British ministry could give the King any hope for Hanover if she should provoke France by following the course of British politics.[10]

After a few initial successes, the allied armies were again beaten by the French even before Napoleon had returned from Egypt to win the decisive battle of Marengo. Russia had already withdrawn from the battlefield because of real or fancied slights to her troops by the Austrians. The peace of Lunéville (9 February 1801) included the Empire as such, while the peace of Campoformio had been made only with Austria. The entire left bank of the Rhine was now formally ceded to France. Austria lost important territories in Italy, while the German princes who had lost lands west of the Rhine were to be compensated with other territories within the Empire. George, as Elector of Hanover, acceded to the treaty of Lunéville only with reluctance, stipulating that it was not to be regarded as a precedent.[11] He was also disinclined to participate in the intense competition that followed among the princes of Germany for the rich pickings — mostly, but not exclusively, ecclesiastical — awaiting distribution. Besides, as he was also King of Britain and therefore an enemy of France, he could not well send a delegation to Paris to negotiate with the French, as other princes, especially Prussia, were doing. As a result, all Hanover was able to acquire at the division of the spoils was an end to the alternation at Osnabruck, which now became part of her territory, but for which she had to give up a district on the Oldenburg border and certain ancient rights in the cities of Hamburg and Bremen. Prussia, on the other hand, obtained such plums as Hildesheim, Paderborn, and Eastern Westfalia, all on the Hanover border, besides many other provinces. There can be little doubt that an Elector resident in the country and not bound by ties to Britain could have done much better for Hanover on this occasion, though Prussia lost all she had gained after only two years. The King was bitterly disappointed at this poor outcome for his Electorate, and let his British ministers feel his displeasure,[12] though the fault was hardly theirs and it is difficult to see how they could have helped him.

Britain was now left to fight the French without allies. Perhaps never before or since has the entire continent of Europe been so united in hostility against Britain as it was at this moment. Britons had long been disliked because of their wealth, their arrogance, and their ruthless pursuit of their trading interests. Hatred and envy of the proud trading nation found a focus when the British refused to return the island of Malta to the Knights of St. John. The knights, many of whom were French, had surrendered their stronghold to Napoleon on his way to Egypt after only a token resistance, and it had taken a siege of two years to drive out the French garrison. It was only natural that Britain would not give up the island while she was still at war with France. Yet not even the worst excesses of the regime of terror in France had aroused such indignation and abhorrence in Europe as was voiced on this occasion. Foremost among Britain's enemies was Paul I of Russia, who had fought the French partly because of Malta, and now felt obliged to attack the British.[13]

Egged on by the Tsar, Prussia made use of this opportunity to occupy Hanover. She justified her action by pointing out that the peace of Lunéville had superseded the treaty of Basel, that the demarcation line was no longer legally in existence, and that it was necessary to protect Hanover against a possible French attack. The Hanoverian ministry sent a delegation under the nominal leadership of the Duke of Cambridge to Berlin in an attempt to forestall the occupation, but in vain. In April they submitted, slavishly thanking the King of Prussia for the gracious utterances in his proclamation of occupation, and imploring his protection.[14] Prussia had joined a league formed on the instigation of Tsar Paul between the northern states for the defence of neutral shipping against the right of search claimed by the British navy. She now closed the mouths of the Weser and the Elbe against British vessels. The British had hitherto spared Prussian ships in an effort to protect Hanover,[15] but now their forbearance came to an end.

The Prussians had hardly established themselves in the Electorate, when they were forced to move out. Tsar Paul had been assassinated in March 1801, after he had orderd his army to conquer India, and was succeeded by his son Alexander I. The new Tsar favoured a reconciliation with Britain, and the northern ports were again opened to British ships. Pressure was put on Prussia to evacuate Hanover as soon as it was clear that there was no danger of a French attack,[16] and by the end of October the country was free again. There was no present threat from France because she was negotiating a peace with Britain. It was concluded at Amiens in March 1802, its terms including the return of all conquered colonial territories, the handing back of Malta to the Knights of St. John, and an end to French aspirations in Egypt.

The Peace of Amiens lasted for just fifteen months. The British were outraged by Napoleon's high-handed conduct in Europe and alarmed by his evident preparations for an attack on their island. They refused to give up Malta because Napoleon was trying to remove the protectorate over the Knights from the Tsar and transfer it to the King of Naples, whom he could influence. War was declared in May 1803, and the French immediately got ready to attack Hanover. As usual, the Electoral ministers were not prepared for defence, although they had been warned of their danger two months before. The army had been reduced to 15000 men under the Prussian occupation, and it was difficult to find recruits, many of whom had come from lands now incorporated into Prussia. When orders came from the King to prepare for war, ministers sent to England for fresh instructions, instead of doing the best they could. True, the orders had been quite vague, leaving practically everything to the discretion of the ministers and the military commander, but this very fact might have spurred a more active ministry to set up some sort of resistance. The invading French consisted mainly of ragged, half-starved levies who were to be outfitted at the expense of Hanover. They did not even have a train of artillery. A determined attempt to oppose the enemy would at the very least have gained some time and might have led to more favourable terms for the Electorate. Preparations for resisting the French were so half-hearted that jokesters claimed the ministry had forbidden the army to shoot at the enemy, and only allowed the soldiers to use the bayonet in cases of extreme necessity, and then with 'Christian moderation'.[17] The ministers could think of nothing better than to ask for Prussian assistance, but they received only an evasive answer.

The Duke of Cambridge, who was nominally in command of the Electoral army, left for England in disgust at the lack of fighting spirit among its generals, and Hanover surrendered practically unconditionally at the convention of Sulingen (3 June 1803). The only concessions the French would make were to allow the army to remain intact on condition the soldiers swore never to fight against France, and to leave the duchy of Lauenburg unoccupied. Even these terms were not ratified by Napoleon, who declared he would only consent to them if Britain set free the French sailors imprisoned in England. At the beginning of the war, the British navy had captured a considerable number of French merchantmen who were unaware of the outbreak of hostilities, and had taken the sailors into captivity. Obviously the British government would not and could not return these men to France. Britain's only hope of victory lay in the superiority of the British navy over the French, and it was out of the question for her to strengthen the enemy by letting France have the use of these trained and experienced seamen. Hanover was forced to conclude a new convention, called the Elbe Convention, according to which the army was to be dissolved, and Lauenburg also to be occupied by the French. Many of the Hanoverian soldiers, who unlike their superior officers had retained their martial spirit, made their way to England, where they were welcomed with open arms. In the confusion which followed the announcement of the Elbe Convention, the administration of the oath not to fight against the French had been overlooked.

For the next two years, Hanover remained under French occupation and suffered severely. British war propaganda spread rumours that the country was subject to unbridled French rapacity and lust, that whole villages were burnt to the ground and women of the highest rank violated in the streets. (Our forefathers' indignation at a crime was proportional to the rank of the victim.) These stories[18] had little or no foundation in fact. The lower ranks of the French army seem to have got on quite well with the inhabitants, and there was no need for them to resort to rape.[19] What bled the country white were the *douceurs* and gratifications demanded by the high-ranking officers, the supplies in kind exacted from the peasants, and the high level of taxation. All in all, the French occupation during these two years is estimated to have cost Hanover 26 million Reichsthalers, or more than five times the annual revenue.[20] The King-Elector's personal property was used as security for huge loans forced on the Hanse towns.

The French occupying troops left Hanover in September 1805 for southern Germany in order to fight the Austrians, who had reluctantly agreed to join a coalition of Britain, Russia, Sweden, and Naples against France. (Albion was no longer detested and was now on her way to becoming the 'Last Citadel of Freedom'.) Napoleon needed only a few months to inflict a crushing defeat on the Austro-Russian army at Austerlitz (2 December 1805) and to occupy Vienna. All hope of effective resistance to the French seemed to have gone, and Austria made what peace she could with the conqueror, losing all territories remaining to her in Italy as well as provinces in southern Germany, including the Tyrol, which had to be ceded to Bavaria. Nelson's even more decisive victory at Trafalgar a few weeks earlier had passed almost unnoticed on the Continent.

On their way south from Hanover, the French troops had marched across Prussian territory without asking for permission. Even after this insult to her sovereignty, Prussia hesitated to join the allies because she still hoped to remain neutral. For the same reason, she had not accepted Napoleon's offer of an alliance, although he promised to give her Hanover if she accepted. Prussia's doubts were resolved by Austerlitz, and she immediately concluded an alliance with France, ceding certain outlying territories against the acquisition of the Electorate. She lost no time in seizing her part of the booty.

After the French had left Hanover, the British had made preparations to reoccupy the country. An Anglo-Hanoverian corps was landed near Cuxhaven, and a Russo-Swedish army crossed the Elbe near Hamburg after Sweden had been awarded a subsidy of £60000. But there were delays and a perhaps not unreasonable reluctance to engage British forces on the Continent at this time, expecially as Napoleon was already forcing the Austrians to retreat. On 2 December 1805, George issued a proclamation to his loyal German subjects stating that the reoccupation of Hanover by his own troops had been delayed by contrary winds, and that in the meantime the King of Prussia would occupy the Electorate 'under the most friendly assurances'. Count Munster was appointed Chief Minister and would attend to civil affairs, while the Duke of Cambridge would be sent to Germany to administer military matters.[21] Some Prussian troops were already stationed in Hanover. They had been the first to fill the vacuum left after the departure of the French and had been greeted joyfully as deliverers by the population, a joy that soon turned to suspicion when it was noted that the Prussians made no attempt to attack the garrison the French had left in the fortress of Hamelin.[22] Once they had concluded their alliance with Napoleon, the Prussians poured more soldiers into the Electorate.

Even before the Duke of Cambridge reached Germany, the King of Prussia had issued a proclamation declaring that he had taken possession of Hanover 'until a general peace' (27 January 1806). Two months later (1 April 1806) he formally annexed the country on the grounds that it was

French by right of conquest, and had been given to Prussia in exchange for other provinces. The mouths of the Elbe and Weser had already been closed to British shipping. Munster left for England protesting at Prussia's action, but exhorting the inhabitants to submit peacefully. As a matter of fact, Prussia, who had no allies except Napoleon, whom she did not really trust, would have preferred a more amicable arrangement with Britain. In December 1805, she had offered George Mecklenburg or some territory in Poland in exchange for Hanover. The King considered this proposal 'strange and insulting' and wrote to Munster that no consideration would cause him to agree to such a measure.[23] Prussia tried again in March 1806, and now offered to let George retain Hanover west of the Weser as well as most of Westfalia if he would cede the rest of the Electorate and a foothold on the west bank of the river.[24] Again the King refused and the British ambassador to Berlin was told to inform the Prussian court that neither political convenience, much less an equivalent or indemnity would ever induce His Majesty to forget 'what is due to his rights and the exemplary fidelity and attachment of His Hanoverian subjects'.

Prussia's annexation of the King's German dominions caused a strong reaction in Britain. Immediately after the Prussian King's declaration of occupation, the Foreign Secretary protested in strong terms to the Prussian minister in London. In a debate on 23 April, Parliament expressed its abhorrence, pity, and contempt for Prussia's action and passed an address to the King affirming that they were willing and determined to defend him. All ports held by Prussia were blockaded and an embargo placed on Prussian shipping.[25] The Prince of Wales published a declaration in His Majesty's name stating that nothing would extinguish the love and attachment the King felt for a people over whom his ancestors had happily reigned for so many centuries and that to the end of his life he would never cease to devote all his efforts to the maintenance and welfare of his Electorate.[26]

All this activity on their behalf did not necessarily please the Hanoverian politicians. After Austerlitz, Napoleon seemed invincible, and any prudent statesman would have wished to come to terms with the conqueror, as all other minor German states had already done. An Electorate independent of Britain under a prince of the ruling house (Hanoverians never for a moment faltered in their loyalty to the Guelfs) might attain the same status as a French protectorate that was enjoyed by Bavaria, Wurttemberg, and others. This aim could only be achieved if the two countries were entirely separate, and Britain gave up all interest in Hanover. But when orders were issued to sink, burn, and destroy all Prussian vessels, this dream was shattered, and the German Chancery resignedly wrote to the Hanoverian envoys who were still at their posts that 'all efforts to separate our interests from those of England have come to nothing'.[27]

In the summer of 1806, only a few months after the Prussians had taken over, it became known that Napoleon was offering to return the Electorate to Britain if a peace could be arranged. Prussia knew her turn to be conquered had come and made desperate efforts to find allies. The Tsar readily promised assistance, while the British made difficulties. The Prussians suggested that their present differences with the British were to be settled by an agreement to be mediated by the Tsar, and that the restitution of Hanover be discussed at a general peace,[28] while trade was to be resumed immediately. The British government would not listen to such proposals, rightly claiming that Hanover would in any case be an object of discussion at a general peace. They were willing to lift the blockade, but only if they received a guarantee that the Electorate would be returned immediately. Even this was not enough for the King, whose failing mind was by now concentrated on Hanover to the exclusion of all else. He insisted that the return of his dominions must go hand in hand with the lifting of the English blockade.[29] To satisfy the King, the cabinet instructed Lord Morpeth, who was to go to Prussia as a special envoy, to tell the Berlin court that the British blockade of Prussia would be lifted for one month and would then be reinstated unless Prussia agreed to the absolute and unconditional restitution of His Majesty's Electoral dominions, such restitution to be effected at a general peace, regardless of its terms. The extraordinary formulation of this instruction was presumably chosen so that ministers could assure the King that they had obeyed his orders to the letter, while at the same time they made certain that Hanover would not be denuded of troops. Before Morpeth could inform the Prussians of these terms, Napoleon had struck. On 14 October 1806, he destroyed the Prussian army at Jena, and Prussia temporarily ceased to be a great power.

Hanover was occupied by French troops and lost her political identity. During the following years, parts of her territory were incorporated into the Kingdom of Westfalia, others into France itself. The people suffered in helpless silence. When there was another war between France and Austria in 1809, and unrest broke out in other parts of Germany, the Hanoverians also were ready to undertake a rising, but they remained quiet on express orders from London.[30] Nevertheless the Duke of Brunswick, who had fought for the Austrians in Saxony, found enough assistance in the country to enable him to flee to the Weser near Bremen and sail thence to England with 2000 fighting men.[31]

Ever since the Elbe Convention of 1803, officers and men of the Hanoverian army had been travelling to England to continue their fight against Napoleon, and soon untrained young men began to follow them. Recruiting offices were set up for them at Harwich and Plymouth. When the number of Hanoverians in England reached a thousand, the 'King's German Legion' was founded by Royal Patent of 19 December 1803. It continued to grow steadily. Braving the death penalty for both recruiters and recruited, thousands of volunteers, often fresh from school, undertook the journey to England, using small boats to reach Heligoland, then a British possession, travelling via neutral Denmark, or by any route available, they crossed the Channel to serve their hereditary monarch. By 1813, the number of legionaries had increased to 16000 men, most of them Hanoverians, with a few other Germans among them. The Legion was treated as a part of the British army and employed everywhere the British fought, among other things at the siege of Copenhagen in 1807, on the ill-fated Schelde (Scheldt) expedition of 1809, in Spain, and on Sicily.[32] At the battle of Waterloo, 5500 legionaries were among the few veteran troops at Wellington's disposal. We also hear of an Anglo-German Legion in the service of Russia,[33] and may safely assume that this too was chiefly composed of Hanoverians. In later years, Hanoverians were able to boast that they were the only Germans who had never stopped fighting Napolean for twelve years.

Count Munster, who had fled to London in 1806, played an important political role that still awaits a biographer (his papers have only been accessible to the public at the Hanover archives since 1978). He soon managed to gain the ear of the King and his son, the Prince of Wales (later the Prince Regent and George IV). While British ministers came and went, Munster stayed on, and many politicians found it useful to cultivate his friendship because he always enjoyed personal access to the monarch, who had full confidence in his integrity and his knowledge of Continental affairs. Foreign potentates and statesmen often preferred to address themselves to Munster, whom they understood and who could understand them, while British politicians often seemed to act irrationally to minds not used to democratic procedures. The reports he received from Hanoverians who had remained at their diplomatic posts in a private capacity often provided valuable information.[34]

11

THE POST-NAPOLEONIC AGE

When the news of Napoleon's defeat in Russia reached
Hanover, the people rose in arms against the French, and
several skirmishes were fought against enemy troops stationed around Hamburg.[1] The hastily assembled levies were
almost untrained and poorly armed, and in spite of a few
minor victories were unable to make an impression on
disciplined soldiers. Deliverance came only after Napoleon
had lost the three-day battle of Leipzig on 18 October 1813,
and had to retreat to France. Two weeks after the battle,
the first allied troops under Crown Prince Bernadotte of
Sweden entered Gottingen, where they were received with
unbounded joy. Bernadotte soon moved on to Hanover city,
where he found an equally enthusiastic welcome. He had
been preceded there by the Duke of Cumberland, who had
acknowledged the cheers and demonstrations of the crowd,
but had otherwise kept in the background. No one could
yet know that twenty years later he would become King of
Hanover. The situation Bernadotte had to deal with was by
no means as rosy as the newly liberated citizens imagined.
There was still an army of 30000 French entrenched round
the fortified city of Hamburg. At any moment they might
attempt to break out to the west and join Napoleon, who
was not finally beaten until the following year. It was
necessary to assemble and train a Hanoverian army.
Fortunately there was no lack of volunteers, and the allied
arsenals could supply sufficient arms. In a short time the

Hanoverian forces, strengthened by some allied troops, could present a formidable appearance, and the French commander, Marshal Davout, preferred not to risk a battle.

From Britain, the Prince Regent now proceeded to take possession of his ancestral domains. British and Hanoverian troops from the German Legion were landed, and on 19 December 1813 the Duke of Cambridge, accompanied by Count Munster, reached Hanover city. The Duke had been appointed Governor General of Hanover, a new post the functions of which still had to be defined, but that clearly signified that henceforth Hanover was to be treated more visibly as an independent country. The new Governor General was a younger brother of the Duke of Cumberland, and the latter was deeply disappointed that Cambridge had been preferred for a post which he had expected to obtain for himself. This advancement of the younger brother over the elder was probably due to the influence of Munster, who was the confidant of the Prince Regent. Munster found it easier to get along with the pliable Duke of Cambridge, who could be reduced to a figurehead, while Cumberland was a man of strong convictions who would have insisted on playing an independent role.

The fate of Europe after Napoleon's abdication was decided at the Congress of Vienna. As soon as it opened, the Prince Regent announced that in future Hanover was to be a kingdom, as its ruler was a member of one of the oldest princely houses in Germany, who could not hold a lesser rank than the new Kings of Bavaria, Wurttemberg, and Saxony. This met with no objections, but determining the frontiers of the new kingdom proved to be more difficult. In 1812, while Prussia was fighting Napoleon and was in need of British subsidies, an agreement had been made with Britain about Hanover, according to which the Electorate was to receive an 'adequate' increase of territory, which would include Hildesheim. At the Peace Congress, Prussia nevertheless tried hard to obtain the entire country, or at least the greater part of it, for herself, while George III was to be compensated elsewhere. Powerful Britain would hear none of this, and Prussia had to give way. Hanoverian territory was enlarged by districts in the south-east (including Hildesheim) and along the river Ems, giving the new kingdom a welcome common frontier with the Netherlands. The Duchy of Lauenburg, on the other hand, had to be given up, and became a part of Danish Schleswig-Holstein. Hanover was now fourth in size and fifth in population among the post-Napoleonic states of Germany and might seem headed for a safe and prosperous future but for one fatal weakness, her geographical position. The kingdom lay athwart the new Prussian dominions, separating the prosperous industrial west from the poorer, agricultural, and more populous east. It could be foreseen that as soon as a suitable opportunity arose, Prussia would not remain content with the two military roads across the country she had a right to use, but would attempt to secure at least a broad land bridge to unite her territories.

Hanover became part of the German Federation (*Deutscher Bund*), a rehash of the old Empire with such changes as were imposed by the new conditions. There was no longer an Emperor, as Prussia demanded an equal voice with Austria in German affairs, and the new kings did not relish a visible sovereign over them either. There was no central court of justice. Further, all member states were now supposed to have a constitution, though this provision was not strictly enforced, and such constitutions as were promulgated were definitely oligarchical. In Hanover, the old unwritten constitution remained in force, altered only by the institution of a central Diet. The Diets of the old historic duchies remained, but soon lost all importance.

Unfortunately for the Hanoverians, the return of the good old times they had hoped for failed to come about. For one thing, the war still had to be paid for, and they soon complained that taxes were just as high as they had been under the French. For another, if they had not enjoyed liberty and fraternity under foreign occupation, they had at least enjoyed equality, for all differences between nobles and commoners had been abolished. People now found the revived privileges of the gentry hard to stomach. The general trade slump that followed the end of the war affected agricultural Hanover less than it did industrial Britain, but still caused much hardship. There was even discontent in the army, because the former members of the King's German Legion considered themselves less favourably treated than they had a right to expect. Officers and NCOs sometimes had to accept posts inferior to those they had held under British command, while others, who had joined the army only at the end of the war were preferred.

The new Diet was opened on 12 December 1814 by the Duke of Cambridge. He told the members that the sovereign demanded nothing for himself (i.e. they would not have to pay taxes to support the London Court) and exhorted them to be to Hanover what Parliament was in the sister kingdom — the high council of the nation.[2] One of the Diet's first actions was to abolish the exemption of the nobles' estates from taxation. The nobles tried to stop the passing of this measure by leaving the hall of assembly and thus preventing a quorum, but enough of them were halted at the exit by physical obstruction to ensure the legality of the vote. This early exercise in democratic procedures did not, however, herald the approach of true democracy. During the following years, Hanover was in effect ruled by Munster. From London, where George IV invariably followed his advice, he kept a tight rein on the government, all important decisions were made by him, and his approval was necessary for all appointments. Munster even tried to transfer the control of financial affairs to London, but had to give up this attempt in the face of strong opposition both from Hanover and from Britain.[3] Hanover never came closer to being governed from Britain than in Munster's time.[4] Yet even Munster did not wish Hanover to be ruled from London permanently. When some Hanoverian politicians — the kingdom now had a political life of its own — suggested that Hanover become part of the British Empire, Munster opposed the idea. He argued that if the country became a British province, it could be ceded at some future peace in exchange for other territories; similar cases had occurred in the past. The present situation was safer for Hanover as Britain had no right to give up her King's inheritance.[5] The Duke of Cambridge, during Munster's ascendancy, remained governor-general only in name, his authority being restricted to military matters, and even here he could do little without Munster's consent.

In the year after his accession to the throne, George IV decided to visit Hanover, and for the first time Hanoverians encountered a monarch who could not speak proper German. The King arrived at Hanover city on 10 September 1821, accompanied by Munster and the Foreign Secretary, having been met on the way by the Dukes of Cumberland and Cambridge. The joy of the population was unbounded. A salute of 101 guns was fired, church bells rang, and innumerable dances and festivities were held. There were military parades, operas, fireworks and torch-light processions. Even an elephant had been brought across the Channel from the royal menagerie for the occasion.[6] Count Munster, well versed in English ways, had given orders to furnish all bedrooms with water-closets, footbaths, and tea-kettles. Anything less would be considered barbarous by the English.[7] There was, however, no coronation ceremony; coronations had already gone out of fashion on the Continent. George did not remain in Hanover for long. Plagued by the gout and yearning for the comforts of London, he cut short his stay in the city and gave up his intention of touring the country. He contented himself with a brief visit to Gottingen, and returned home via Cologne and Brussels. By 7 November, he had already reached Calais. He had plans to make another visit to the Continent in 1822, and this time travel as far as Austria, Hungary, and Saxony, but these came to nothing, although preparations for his visit were begun.[8]

In 1824, a report reached England that Hanover had concluded a concordat with the Pope, and had granted full civil rights to the adherents of the Catholic religion. This was a gross misrepresentation of the facts. All Hanover had done was to persuade the Pope to issue a bull by which the sees of the Catholic bishops were rearranged to coincide with the new political frontiers and publish it in the *Official Gazette*. A concordat had been refused by the Hanoverians because the Pope's conditions were found too onerous. Nor had any new rights been granted to Catholics: liberty of conscience had long been the rule in Hanover, and was now even more imperative as the country had acquired a sizeable Catholic minority and tolerance was imposed by the laws of the German Federation. In England, this was the time when the question of Catholic Emancipation, i.e. the freeing of Catholics from the many civil disabilities imposed on them, was being hotly debated. Under these circumstances the garbled news from Hanover caused great excitement. Hotheads declared that the dynasty was trying to introduce Catholic Emancipation through the back door, and even that there were plans to turn Britain into a Catholic country again. The issue was debated in Parliament. The Prime Minister, Lord Liverpool, found it necessary to approach the King about the matter. George wrote to him that he had had no knowledge of the intention to publish what he called the Catholic declaration, and that he shared his father's views against the emancipation of Catholics. He did not write that he had agreed to the bull itself and ought to have known that it would be published.[9]

Emotions in England had hardly calmed down when O'Connell, the defender of Irish rights, made a speech in Parliament declaring that the British government, through His Majesty's Hanoverian minister to Rome, had three times applied to the Pope for a concordat, but had been refused because the Pope had made the emancipation of Catholics a prior condition to any agreement. The speech was reported in *The Times* of 22 November 1828, and caused general consternation. The Duke of Wellington, the new Prime Minister, asked the King to insist that Munster publicly contradict this falsehood, and did not declare himself satisfied until Munster had obtained a full report from the Hanoverian envoy to Rome denying the allegation.[10]

After the French July revolution in 1830, widespread unrest broke out in many parts of Germany. In Hanover, the disturbances were almost exclusively confined to the town of Gottingen and its university. They were easily put down when, after some delay, the military intervened. But the authorities professed to be worried and made representations to the Duke of Cambridge, alleging that there was general disquiet in the country and that the army was too weak to suppress any more widespread uprising. They asked that the people be appeased by introducing more democracy and granting greater powers to the Diet. The real reason for their representations was not so much the trouble at Gottingen, as the dissatisfaction of the civil servants, by now largely recruited from the middle classes, with Munster's autocratic rule. The Duke passed the complaints on to the King; Munster was dismissed, and a new written constitution embodying more liberal principles was proclaimed. The Duke of Cambridge was appointed Viceroy with full regal powers. The Duke of Cumberland was merely informed of the changes without being asked for his approval, although it was now becoming apparent that he would one day become King of Hanover. Perhaps it was known that he would have objected to some features of the new constitution, especially the transfer of the crown lands to the state, the monarch being provided instead with a civil list on the British model.

As soon as the waves of the July revolution had subsided, the German Federation, under the influence of the Austrian Chancellor Metternich, issued a series of restrictive orders which included rigorous censorship of the press, the prohibition of political meetings, restraints on foreigners at universities, and the principle that the states composing the Federation should watch each others' political conduct. These orders were embodied in the Frankfurt Protocol of 13 July 1832, and were proclaimed by the Duke of Cambridge in the name of his brother, King William IV, (who had succeeded George IV in 1830) and after obtaining his consent. The proclamation caused considerable disquiet and animosity among liberal-minded Germans. On the Continent, the voice of Hanover was still considered the voice of Britain, and it had been hoped that Britain would help to defend Germany's liberties. As a matter of fact, Palmerston, then Foreign Secretary, had attempted to persuade the King to prevent the publication of the Frankfurt Protocol, but the King had told him not to meddle in Hanover affairs.

King William never visited Hanover as King, although he knew the country well, having spent many years there as a youth. At the beginning of his reign he was unable to leave England because his presence was required during the agitation about the Great Reform Bill of 1832, and later he became too old and infirm to undertake the journey. In any case the Royal House was already represented by the Duke of Cambridge as Viceroy. But William continued to take an interest in Hanoverian affairs. We are told that even on his death bed, he overruled the wishes of his attendants and insisted on seeing the Hanoverian minister, Baron von Ompteda.[11] As William's end drew near, there were rumours current that the Duke of Cumberland considered himself more suited for the British throne than his niece Victoria, and would seize power by a coup after the King's death.[12] But although it is quite probable that the Duke would have liked to become King of Great Britain and may have thought himself better qualified than the young princess, there is no real evidence that he ever seriously thought of ascending the throne by force.

On 20 June 1837, William died, and the Personal Union came to an end, as females could not succeed in Hanover while any male members of the royal house were alive. Amid the rejoicings at the accession of Victoria, the end of the relationship with Hanover was forgotten. Few London newspapers took notice of the separation, and 'none of them with regret — a fresh illustration of the little value attached in this country to foreign dominion as a source of wealth or strength', as the Annual Register put it. Princes and peers signed an act of allegiance to the new Queen, the first name on the document being 'Ernest Augustus, King of Hanover'.

The new King lost no time in setting out for his kingdom. He had always been actively disliked in England, where he had been accused of almost every crime in the book, including murder, incest, and arson, though nothing was ever proved against him. His popularity was not enhanced by an ugly scar from a wound he had received while fighting in the Netherlands, which forced him to wear high, stiff collars in order to keep his head straight. There was so much hostility against him that according to rumour, the Duke of Wellington told him to 'get out or be pelted'.

In Hanover, feelings after the change were more mixed. Hanoverians were proud of regaining full independence, but had fears for their future without British protection. These thoughts were overshadowed by their anxiety about the future conduct of the new King, as he was known to have a strictly conservative outlook. The Duke of Cambridge, on the other hand, had been much beloved by the people, and before his departure the burghers of Hanover visited his palace dressed in black to show their sorrow.

King Ernest Augustus turned out not to be as bad as he had been painted. He did indeed, after some thought, abrogate the constitution of 1832 on 30 October 1837, but it was not his intention to introduce authoritarian government. The change merely meant that the old constitution came back into force. All the King wanted was to regain the crown lands and an independent income, for he thought it was not in accordance with his royal dignity to have to rely on a civil list. (It later turned out that he would have done better to keep to the 1832 arrangement.) Ernest Augustus was still the next in line of succession to the British throne, and Palmerston thought it necessary to make inquiries about the constitutional change.[13] He was told to mind his own business. A few years later, a new constitution for Hanover was promulgated, and the King adhered to it faithfully until he was forced to make greater concessions in the aftermath of the French February revolution of 1848. By then, he was an old man, and even a younger one might have had to give way.

Understandably, Ernest Augustus had little love for England once he had become King. He was a great admirer of Prussia, where he had lived for many years. During the first year of his reign, he abolished the beloved red coats the Hanoverian soldiers had worn even before the Personal Union, and substituted Prussian blue. He followed this up by gradually reforming the army according to the Prussian model. The old traditions were however maintained, and Hanoverians continued to be proud of the victories of Minden, Salamanca, and Waterloo. But the British share in these battles was more and more overlooked, and Hanoverian youths grew up in the belief that it was their fathers who had done most of the fighting. The legend of 'the Germans to the front' arose, with the implication that whenever the British had found themselves in a tight corner, they had called on the Hanoverians to help them out. No time or place for such an incident was mentioned at first, but the story grew with the telling, and soon spread all over Germany. It was still alive during the Second World War, when the fighting in Spain had long been forgotten, and the event was supposed to have taken place during the Chinese Boxer rebellion, where actually the Germans did not fight at all.

When Queen Victoria married and her children were born, all hopes Ernest Augustus may have retained of becoming King of Britain disappeared. Although he never learned to speak or write correct German, he became — quite properly of course — a purely German prince. He only returned to England once, in 1843. At first he was delighted to see the scenes of his childhood again and even took up his seat in the House of Lords. For a time, he was the lion of the season, but he was not well received at Court, and soon went back to Hanover, not without first picking a quarrel with Prince Albert over a point of precedence.[14] He died in 1851, succeeded by his son, George V of Hanover.

When war broke out between Austria and Prussia in 1866, Hanover sided with the Austrians. On 26 June of that year, the Hanoverian army fought and won its last battle, but had to surrender the next day, surrounded by more numerous and better-armed Prussian troops. Hanover became a Prussian province, and the personal property of the Guelfs was put under sequester. George V did not return to Britain, where he had spent many years as a youth and lost the sight of one eye at Kew, leading to his total blindness in later years, but preferred to retire to Austria. When he died on a journey to Paris in 1878, his body was taken to England and interred in Windsor Chapel on the orders of his cousin Victoria.

Hanoverians had at first strongly objected to becoming Prussian subjects, but the rising tide of German nationalism, increased economic prosperity, the appearance of new ideas, especially socialism, and Prussia's undeniable skill in assimilating new German subjects, soon made the memory of the Guelfs begin to fade. A Guelf party (*Deutsch-Hannoversche Partei*) true to the dynasty was indeed formed, and managed to get representatives elected to the Prussian Diet and the German Reichstag, but never gained real influence. In practice, the party's activity was limited to the dispatching of loyal addresses to the heirs of the Guelfs on suitable occasions such as birthdays and marriages.

The Hanoverian crown jewels were smuggled to England in 1867, most of them under a lady's petticoats. They were later taken to Austria, then to Germany, and finally brought out of the Soviet occupation zone in 1945 under the protection of a British convoy. They are now in a bank vault, unseen symbols of an all but forgotten kingdom.

Most of the archives of the German Chancery were brought to Hanover in 1837, and the rest followed some years later. Ernest Augustus, after having them checked, ordered about two-thirds of the papers to be burnt, possibly destroying much information we would have liked to have had about the relations of the people of Hanover with the London court and with England. The remaining papers are still carefully preserved, while the archives of the Hanoverian ministry of foreign affairs were lost in a fire during the Second World War.

I2

CONCLUSION

F. von Ompteda, writing only a few years after the end of the Personal Union, was probably the first to remark that 'never in history has the principle of a purely personal union been so consistently put into practice as in the case of England and Hanover'.[1] The observation is still true today, and likely to remain so until personal unions should once more become fashionable. Though there were exceptions, such as the two occasions when Hanoverian troops were ordered out of the country to defend Britain and her Empire, the relationship between the two countries was always essentially personal, and nothing held them together except the fact that they had a common monarch. One may wonder why two governments placed in such a situation which could last for centuries did not make an attempt to provide some sort of institution which might enable them to cooperate more efficiently. There were three chief reasons why no effort was ever made in this direction: the policy of the Hanoverian Kings of Britain; the attitude of British politicians; and the position of the Hanoverian ministers.

All the kings of the Guelf dynasty, probably including George IV, were averse to a closer union between the two countries under their rule and especially jealous of British interference in Hanover affairs. For George I and George II, the motive was the wish to preserve their homeland from foreign domination. For George III, Hanover was a country where he was safe from the political struggles he had to face at home, where his orders were never questioned, and where his ministers did not have to take into account the wishes of an elected parliament. William IV was well acquainted with Hanover, having lived there for many years, and knew that the connection with Britain would come to an end after his death. None of these monarchs could bear the thought of his German territory being administered by the British. Hanoverian and British ministers were told many times that they must not express opinions on any matter that did not concern their own country, that the King did not take English ministers' advice on Empire affairs, nor Electoral ministers' advice on English business.[2]

British ministers had grown up in a nation that was not interested in Hanover, and where a knowledge of Hanoverian affairs was not helpful to their careers. Usually, they were confronted with the problems posed by the Personal Union only after they had attained high office. Accustomed to see politics in the context of what was already a worldwide empire, they tended to despise Hanover as an insignificant little country and to forget about it when there was peace in Europe. In times of tension they found the Electorate on the one hand an impediment to British policy because it could not be allowed to fall into enemy hands, and on the other a useful asset, because Hanover was a reliable ally who could be trusted to provide loyal and well-trained troops for the defence of vital British interests on the Continent. No one ever developed a clearcut policy to solve this dilemma. Carteret did indeed once consider uniting Hanover with Britain, but he seems to have given up this idea very soon. British attitude towards Hanover was thus always determined on a pragmatic basis, politicians doing what the exigencies of the moment demanded, and no more.

This lack of a coherent British policy made things very difficult for the ministers in Hanover. Trained to unquestioning obedience to their monarch, but for many years unable to consult or advise him personally, they were unable to form a consistent political strategy, a fact which makes it problematic to write the history of the Personal Union from a Hanoverian viewpoint. The ministers often had to contend with sudden shifts of attitude in Britain which seemed inexplicable to them. They knew of course that such shifts were generally caused by the exigencies of British politics, but they did not understand the motives behind the changes. These were often difficult to comprehend in any case, as British policy was subject to a variety of influences, such as the state of the political parties and British interests outside Europe. Hanoverians had experience only of the situation within the Empire and its relations with its immediate neighbours. Under such circumstances, ministers tended to withdraw into the world they knew, and preserve it as well as they could, a perhaps not unnatural attitude to adopt for the landed aristocrats they all were. They were aware that Britain had to defend them against their enemies, but had no wish to form closer ties with their protector and become second-class citizens of the British Empire.

The relationship between the two countries was thus an uneasy one, with both sides trying to keep as far apart as possible, yet inevitably being drawn together by the fact of the Personal Union. From a modern point of view there can be little doubt that Hanover, at least, would have benefitted from the appointment of an ambassador in London. The work of a diplomat is based on his intimate knowledge both of his home country and the country to which he is accredited. He can observe developments in the host country, explain them to politicians at home, and often make predictions about future developments. He can also bring his ministry's wishes and suggestions to the attention of the authorities at the post where he is stationed. The Hanoverian minister attached to the king's person could not carry out this function, chiefly because he had no official status with regard to British ministers, who would have found it very strange to hear utterances from the king's servant which were not his master's. Nor could the resident minister write to Hanover on his own. It would further not have been in accordance with the spirit of the age to have a monarch appoint an ambassador to himself and even more unthinkable to have one group of his servants communicating with another behind his back. We know only of one instance of direct communication between British and

Hanoverian ministers on political matters: in 1755, New-castle wrote a letter to his personal friend Munchhausen in which he explained the reasons why Britain felt unable to involve herself in a large-scale war on the Continent, made suggestions for Hanoverian defence, and held out the prospect of financial aid. Not all Munchhausen's letters have been preserved, and it is reasonable to assume that Newcastle was replying to a request from the chief minister.[3]

On the whole it may be said that Hanover derived considerable benefit from the Personal Union. While almost every other part of Germany, especially the neighbouring territories of Westfalia, Thuringia, and Hesse were overrun by enemy troops several times during the course of the eighteenth century, Hanover was occupied only once, for a few months in 1757. While it is quite possible that an Elector of Hanover who was not also King of Great Britain could have succeeded in obtaining Bremen and Verden at the end of the Great Northern War, it would have been difficult for him to defend himself against Prussian ambitions during the decades that followed. Quite probably, the Electorate would have suffered the fate of Mecklenburg and Saxony during the Seven Years' War, when Frederick II used these supposedly neutral territories both as a recruiting ground and a source of revenue, exploiting them ruthlessly. Hanover was indeed left undefended during the time of Napoleon's ascendancy, but her fate was no different from that of all continental Europe outside Scandinavia and the Turkish Empire. At the time, Britain was fighting desper-ately for her own survival, and the suggestion of some Hanoverian historians that their country ought to have been protected by the British cannot be taken seriously.

It is likely that the presence of a foreign dynasty on the British throne had a positive influence on the development of the British constitution. While her kings were still somewhat unsure of their position, and their attention was in part diverted to another country, Britain could develop cabinet government under a prime minister and increase the power of Parliament more quickly than might have been the case under native monarchs. The trend towards greater democracy was, however, already irreversible when the

Guelfs came to the throne. In view of the fate of Charles I and James II, not even a protestant Stuart would have attempted the introduction of Continental-style absolutism in the Kingdom. Otherwise, Britain derived little profit from the Hanoverian connection. True, the Electorate was a dependable ally who provided excellent troops, but the same can nearly always be said of other German states, especially of Hesse. Even without the Personal Union, Britain would surely have been able to find the Continental support she needed against France. No attempt was ever made to exploit Hanover financially, although such a course would have been not at all unusual in the eighteenth century. The reason was presumably that Hanover was too poor a country, and the obstacles, both from the King and Parliament, too great for anyone to be tempted to make such a dishonourable proposal.

Was the Personal Union merely an episode in history, or has it left any trace which can still be discerned today? It is unlikely that the connection with Hanover had any influence on British history. Surely Britain would have acquired a colonial empire in the eighteenth and nineteenth centuries and lost it again in the twentieth, under some other dynasty than the Guelfs. Nor can the Union have had much effect on the history of Hanover, as the little country was undoubtedly fated sooner or later to become a province of some larger German state. Any chance it may have had of becoming the leader of such a state had been lost long before the Personal Union, when Brandenburg-Prussia acquired the bishopric and fortress of Minden at the Peace of Westfalia in 1648.

On the other hand, the Personal Union may have had a lasting effect on the history of Germany. There are at least three different occasions when events might have taken a different course, dependent on whether the ruler of Hanover was or was not also King of Britain. In 1740, Frederick II of Prussia, when his chance came with the death of the Emperor Charles VI, might well have sent his troops across his western frontier instead of attacking powerful Austria. He had shown great interest in western Germany immediately after his accession, and in Hanover pretexts for an attack were even easier to find and pickings even better than in Silesia. He may have decided that a small state backed by a potent king would prove more difficult to overcome than a large one ruled by what he believed to be a weak queen. Again, it is certain that at the Congress of Vienna in 1815, Prussia would have insisted on obtaining at least half of Hanover in order to unite her western and eastern provinces, if Britain had not protected her king's patrimony.

No one can tell whether Bismarck would have hesitated to invade and annex Hanover in 1866 if her King had still been King of Great Britain. But even if he had done so, he would hardly have dared to embark on the following war with France which led, much against the King of Prussia's wishes, to the foundation of the German Empire. The absorption of Hanover would have alienated British public opinion, and Prussia could not risk fighting both France and Britain. It is tempting, but futile, to speculate on the different course German and European history could have taken if the Hohenzollerns had achieved their dream of a north German empire at a time when the south German states might have sought Austrian protection, and Austria had been strong enough to afford it.

REFERENCES

For abbreviations see bibliography, page 186.

Chapter 1

1. BL Add. MSS. 32874, passim.
2. The description of eighteenth-century England is based on the writings of professors Hatton, Plumb, Ward and Williams, and on the 'English Historical Documents'.

Chapter 2

1. PRO SP 81, 161.
2. Schnath, pp.514 ff.
3. Han. Cal. Br. 24, 5133, 27-8-01.
4. ibid., 17-1-11.
5. Vienna, 13-2-14.
6. Hatton, pp.107 f.
7. BL Stowe MSS, 242, fol. 124 ff.
8. ibid., fol. 145 ff.
9. The description of Hanover is based on von Meier and the introduction to von Lenthe, the description of the Holy Roman Empire on Oestreich.

Chapter 3

1. Hatton, pp.134 f.
2. Vienna, 20-4-15.
3. Hatton, p.130.
4. Melville, vol. II, p.11.
5. Bonet, Michael, vol. I, pp.444 ff.; Vienna, 22-2-15.
6. Vienna, 16-9-15.
7. Bonet, Michael, vol. I, pp.709 ff.; Vienna, 21-5-15.
8. Han. Cal. Br. 24, 678, 11/22-3-15.
9. Han. Cal. Br. 24, 677, 16 and 18-3-15.
10. Han. Cal. Br. 24, 678, 5/16-4-15.

11. BL Add. MSS, 28154, 10-5-15.
12. ibid., 6-5-15.
13. Michael, vol. I, p.720.
14. BL Add. MSS, 28154, fol. 56 ff.
15. PRO SP 75, 35, 2-6-15.
16. Han 92, LXVIII 4e, 15-7-15, 27-7-15; Cal. Br. 24, 1426, *passim*.
17. Han. Cal. Br. 24, 1426, 3-9-15.
18. ibid., 17/28-7-15.
19. BL Add. MSS, 28154, 31-7-15.
20. Han. Cal. Br. 24, 1426, 3-9-15.
21. PRO SP 75, 35, 22-10, 2-11, 5-11-15.
22. Hist. MSSC, Townshend papers, 10-5-16.
23. Hist. MSSC, Polwarth papers I, p.75.
24. Mediger, Meckl. pp.206 ff.
25. Han. Cal. Br. 24, 1430, 6-10-16.
26. Hist. MSSC, Polwarth papers I, pp.82 ff.
27. ibid., p.91.
28. BL Add. MSS, 28154, 10-10-16.
29. BL Eg. MSS, 3124, 25-9-16.
30. Han. Cal. Br. 24, 1717, 3-11-16.
31. PRO SP 43, 1, f.130.
32. PRO SP 90, 7, 9/20-10-16.
33. Sbornik, vol. 25, pp.449 f.
34. Genzel, p.143.
35. Han. Cal. Br. 24, 7616, 4/15-7-49 and ibid., 7621, same date.
36. PRO SP 95, 24, 12-7-19.
37. BL Add. MSS, 28146, 4-7-19.
38. PRO SP 78, 164, 2-7-19.
39. PRO SP 95, 25, 20-10-19.
40. Han. 92, LXVI, 12a.
41. Chance, p.487.
42. Marburg, 4fE 187, 11-4-21.

Chapter 4

1. Han. 92 LXXI 6a, 29-11-15.
2. Han. Cal. Br. 24, 1717, 14/25-9-16.
3. Vienna, 6-11-16; 1-12-16.
4. Han. Cal. Br. 24 1717, 23-10-16; 3-11-16.
5. BL Eg. MSS, 3124, 2-10-16.
6. ibid., 25-9-16.
7. BL Add. MSS, 41683, 9-10-16.
8. BL Eg. MSS, 3124, 16-10-16.
9. Vienna, 23-4-17.
10. Vienna, 3-3-19.
11. PRO SP 80, 26, 5-8-18.
12. Han. 92 LXVIII 2f, 11/22-7-18.
13. Williams, Stanhope, p.361.
14. BL Add. MSS, 32686, 24-11-19.

Chapter 4 (continued)

15. Hist. MSSC, Portland MSS V, pp.594ff.
16. ibid.
17. ibid.
18. ibid., and Cowper, pp.162, 168.
19. PRO SP 90, 21, 20/31-12-26.

Chapter 5

1. PRO FO 34,5, 5-12-13.
2. PRO SP 108, 141 and 257.
3. BL Stowe MSS 249.
4. e.g. Han. 92 LXVI 14, 14-8-42.
5. Hannoverscher Staatskal. 1820.
6. Ellis, pp.560ff.
7. Han. 92 IV 4.
8. RA 17169b and 17170b.
9. von Lenthe, p.54.
10. Brauer, p.187.
11. von Lenthe, p.170.
12. Brauer, p.187.
13. Marburg, 4fE, 198ff, *passim*.
14. The description of the Hanover administration is based on von Meier and the introduction to von Lenthe.
15. Drögereit, p.98.
16. BL Stowe MSS 249.
17. The following paragraph is based on Drögereit, pp.115ff. I have not been able to verify his source.
18. Wolfenbuttel, 1 Alt 22, 434, fol. 3 and 5.
19. Drögereit, p.124.
20. Han. 92 III A, 3-3-44.
21. ibid., 27-9-57.

Chapter 6

1. Vienna, 16-1-41.
2. Han. 92 LXXV 13.
3. Vienna, 29-8-27.
4. Marburg, 4fE 220, 13/22-3-37.
5. BL Add. MSS 32751, 6-7-27.
6. Wolfenbuttel, 1 Alt 22, 458.
7. Wolfenbuttel, 1 Alt 22, 434, fol. 19.
8. Wolfenbuttel, 1 Alt 534, 3 and 16-9-27, cf. 1 Alt 3, 28.
9. Han. 92 III A 7b 1, 30-11/9-12-27.
10. Vienna, 20-1-28.
11. Vienna, Vorträge, Kat. 27.
12. Han. Cal. Br. 24, 4402, fol. 76 and 132.
13. Marburg, 4fE 204, 16-2-31.
14. Devonshire Diary, p.42.
15. Ann. Reg. 1772, pp.189ff.

16. Wolfenbuttel 1 Alt, 22, 434, fol. 26 and 44.
17. Braubach, p.123.
18. Coxe, Walpole, vol. 2, p.689.
19. PRO SP 90, 24, 14/25-8-29.
20. Marburg, 4fE 198, 11/22-9-30.
21. The two foregoing paragraphs are based on Du Bourgay's reports in PRO SP 90, 24-26, and the Townshend-Newcastle correspondence in SP 43, 18. Schilling brings more details, but is sometimes unreliable.
22. Marburg, 4fE 203, 29-12-34 (Reply to Pr. Eugene's letter).
23. Patzek, p.10.
24. Han. 92 LVIII 8, 22-8-40.
25. ibid., 9-12-40.
26. PRO SP 90, 48, 6-12-40.
27. Han. 92 LVIII 8, 30-12-40.
28. Han. 92 LXXI 17b, 17-1-41.
29. ibid., 10-2-41 and memorial of same date.
30. Han. 92 LVIII 8, 2-2-41.
31. ibid., 28-2-41 and 3-3-41.
32. Han. 92 LXXI 17b. 7/18-4-41.
33. Vienna, 10-1-41, 27-1-41.
34. PRO SP 80, 144, 27-2-41; SP 80, 145, 17-4-41.
35. PRO SP 80, 144, 31-3-41.
36. PRO SP 43, 28, 5-5-41.
37. cf. Vienna, 3-5-41.
38. Han. Cal. Br. 11, 1978, 15-7-41.
39. BL Add. MSS 35407, 14-7-41; 31-7-41.
40. PRO SP 43, 29, 2-8-41; 9/20-8-41.
41. BL Add. MSS 35407, 19-8-41.
42. PRO SP 43, 29, 2-8-41.
43. cf. Han. 92 LXXI 17b, 28-9-41; BL Add. MSS 35839, fol. 39.
44. Griffith, p.183.
45. BL Add. MSS 32697, 24-8-41.
46. ibid.
47. Han. 92 LXXI 17b, 18-8-41.
48. Vienna, 4-9-41.
49. Dann, p.43.
50. Vienna, 27-11-44.
51. cf. Vienna, 1-9-44, 13-10-44.
52. PRO SP 80, 147, 2-9-41.
53. PRO SP 43, 29.
54. Han. 92 LXXI 17d, 22 and 26-2-42.
55. PRO SP 80, 152, 20-7-42, BL Add, MSS 22529, 28-5-42.
56. BL Add. MSS 22531, 30-3 and 27-4-42.
57. Han. 92 LXXI 17d, 10-6-42.
58. Frederick, vol. II, 19-11-42.
59. PRO SP 90,55, 22 and 24-12-42.
60. Han. 92 LXXI 17d, 23-2-42, 27-3-42.
61. BL Add. MSS 32701, 24-10-42.
62. PRO SP 87, 12, 9/20 and 30-7-42.

63. ibid., 10/21-9 and 12-10-42.
64. Brauer, pp.131ff.
65. Brandis, p.135.
66. BL Add. MSS 32701, fol. 89.
67. PRO SP 87, 12, 11-6-43.
68. BL Add. MSS 35407, 24-6/5-7-43.
69. Gent's Mag. 1744, pp.297ff., 352ff., 460ff.
70. Han. 92 LXXV No. 6.
71. Braubach, Vom Westfälischen . . . p.136.
72. Marshall, p.199.
73. Frederick, vol. III, p.193.
74. PRO SP 80, 165, 3-10 & 7-11-44, cf. Hist. MSSC, Denbigh MSS, p.245.
75. Frederick, vol. III, 21-4-44; 18-12-44.
76. PRO SP 80, 164, 11-9-44.
77. Marshall, pp.198ff.
78. PRO SP 43, 37, 12-7-45; Han. 9d 42, 6-7-45.
79. PRO SP 43, 36, 14-6-45.
80. PRO SP 80, 170, 18-12-45.
81. Brauer, p.174.

Chapter 7

1. Coxe, Pelham, p.429.
2. BL MSS Index, vol. VII, p.251.
3. Han. Cal. Br. 11, 2282, 8-7-53.
4. BL Add. MSS 35480, 21-2-56.
5. PRO SP 90, 64, 11/22-6-48.
6. Mediger, Moskau, pp.446ff.
7. ibid., pp.452f. and 458f.
8. Frederick, vol. XI, pp.249ff. and 334ff.
9. ibid., pp.105f.
10. ibid., p.345.
11. ibid., pp.418ff.
12. Dusseldorf, Kurköln VII, 195/1.
13. Frederick, vol. XII, pp.59 and 95.
14. BL Add. MSS 35480, 21-2-56.
15. Frederick, vol. XII, pp.329ff.
16. Mediger, Moskau, pp.558 and 631.
17. Treue, pp.47ff.
18. Han. Cal. Br. 24, 4510 and 4512, passim; Curiosa Relaçam.
19. Han. 92 LXXII 5a, 29-4-57.
20. Portzek, p.72.
21. BL Add. MSS 6831, fol. 11ff., Add. MSS 6870, fol. 89.
22. cf. Han. 92 LXXII 7a, 4-2-57.
23. Yorke, vol. III, p.164.
24. PRO SP 90, 69, 16-9-57.
25. Han. 92 LXXII 5a, 4-8, 24-8, 13-9, 22-9-57.
26. Yorke, vol. III, pp.186ff.

27. Ann. Reg. 1757, p.229.
28. Frederick, vol. XV, pp.318, 357, 455.
29. Han. 92 LXXXV 12, 26-10-57
30. PRO SP 90, 71, 10-10-57; BL Add. MSS 32874, fol. 475.
31. Devonshire Diary, pp.31 and 36; BL Add. MSS 32898, fol. 284ff.
32. Han. 92 LXVIII, 30, 17-8-62.
33. Ann. Reg. 1760, pp.51ff.
34. Recueil, vol. XVI p. XCVI.
35. Frederick, vol. XX, pp.76 and 156ff.
36. PRO SP 90, 77, 16-1-61.
37. ibid., passim.
38. PRO SP 90, 78, 18-9-61.
39. PRO SP 90, 79, 26-2-62.
40. Mitchell papers, vol. II, pp.254ff.
41. Frederick, vol. XXII, pp.424f., 468.
42. Berlin, Rep. 92, No. 396.

Chapter 8

1. Brooke, pp.162f.
2. Han. 92, IV 101.
3. e.g. Han. 92 LXVI, No. 6.
4. ibid., 13-9-70.
5. Hist. Mus., p.53.
6. Conrady, p.190.
7. Aspinall, vol. I, p.496.
8. Vienna, 25-10-85.
9. Han. 92, XXI, IV, 31-10-69.
10. This paragraph is based on Conrady, pp.181-185.
11. Aspinall, vol. II, p.590.
12. Vienna, 5-8, 9-8, 30-8-74; Han. Cal. Br. 11, 2347, 27-7, 16-8-74.
13. Han. ibid., 20-1-75.
14. Ann. Reg. 1776, pp.64ff.
15. ibid., pp.80ff.
16. Han. 38 C 1, 1-6 and 11-6-81.
17. Aspinall, vol. II, p.177; cf. Marburg, 4fE 334, 22-11-85.
18. Vienna, 25-5-85 et seq.; cf. Leeds, p.115.
19. PRO FO 65, 13, 16-8-85.
20. ibid., 11-10-85.
21. PRO FO 64, 8, 16-8, 2-9, 10-9, 17-9-85.
22. Ann. Reg. 1786, pp.91ff.
23. Salomon, pp.240ff.
24. Hist. MSSC, Dropmore MSS, vol. 7, 27-8-05.

Chapter 9

1. Hist Mus., p.81.
2. von Meier, p.132.
3. Hist. Mus., p.74.

4. von Meier, p.127.
5. Haase, pp.114 and 117.
6. Hannoverscher Staatskal. 1820.
7. Hist. Mus., p.80.
8. Han. 92 LXVI 5a II.
9. Hist. Mus., p.82.
10. Püster, pp.121ff.; Han. 91, Hattorf, No. 62.
11. Baasch, p.181.
12. Püster, pp.138ff.
13. ibid., pp.175ff.
14. ibid., p.106.
15. Ulbricht, pp.46ff.
16. ibid., pp.265ff.
17. Püster, pp.212ff.
18. Ulbricht, pp.231ff.; Püster, pp.211ff.
19. Han. 92 XXI, No. 11.
20. Hist. Mus., p.72.
21. Dann, pp.1f.
22. Ulbricht, p.205.

Chapter 10

1. Braubach, Von der französischen . . . pp.10ff., Sieske, p.6.
2. Treue, pp.110ff.
3. ibid., p.126.
4. Aspinall, vol. 2, pp.309ff.
5. ibid., p.333.
6. ibid., p.360.
7. ibid., p.393.
8. Ann. Reg. 1795, p.262.
9. Ann. Reg. 1797, pp.417, 431, 434ff.
10. Hist. MSSC, Dropmore MSS, vol. 6, p.275.
11. Ann. Reg. 1801, p.280.
12. Hist. MSSC, Dropmore MSS, vol.7, p.111.
13. Treue, p.138; Braubach, Von der französischen . . . p.55.
14. Han. Cal. Br. 24, 1005, 5-4-01.
15. Havemann, p.326.
16. Ann. Reg. 1801, pp.364ff.
17. Sieske, p.41.
18. Ann. Reg. 1803, p.257; Gent's Mag., p.676.
19. von Hassell, pp.340ff.
20. Heinemann, p.324.
21. Ann. Reg. 1805, pp.518ff.
22. Havemann, p.342.
23. Han. 110 A 47, 6-12, 13-12, 27-12-05.
24. PRO FO 64, 17-3-06.
25. Ann. Reg. 1806, pp.173ff.
26. Vienna, 17-6-06.
27. Han. 92 LXVI 8, 3-6-06.

28. Han. 110 A 47, undated memoir by Munster.
29. Aspinall, vol. IV, pp.471, 480.
30. Brandes, p.13, cf. Han. 110 A 51, 1-5-10.
31. Havemann, p.364.
32. Wersebe, pp.230ff.
33. Han. 110 A 104.
34. Brandes, pp.1ff., cf. article 'Munster' in *Allgemeine Deutsche Biographie*.

Chapter 11

1. Havemann, pp.370ff.
2. Ann. Reg. 1814, pp.102ff., 12-8-14.
3. Wellington, vol. 5, p.622.
4. von Meier, pp.190ff.
5. Gruner, p.87.
6. Gent's Mag., 1821, p.365.
7. Hist. Mus., p.60.
8. Gent's Mag., 1822, p.362.
9. Wellington, vol. 2, p.418; Han. 110 A 56, 2-6-24.
10. ibid., vol. 5, p.285.
11. Ann. Reg. 1837, p.374.
12. Ziegler, p.269.
13. Willis, Ernst August, p.135.
14. ibid., p.319.

Chapter 12

1. von Ompteda, p.5.
2. e.g. Han. Cal. Br. 11, 2032, 29-1/9-2-42 and Han. 92 LXXII 5a, 22-11-57.
3. BL Add. MSS 32857, 18-5-55, cf. 2-6 and 2-8-55.

BIBLIOGRAPHY

Books and manuscripts (MSS) are listed below according to the abbreviations used under References, see pages 178-185.

Unpublished manuscript sources

Berlin   *Preussisches Staatsarchiv*, Berlin. (The bulk of the Prussian archives is kept in the former German Democratic Republic and was inaccesible at the time of writing.)
BL   British Library, Manuscript Division.
Dusseldorf   *Nordrhein-Westfälisches Staatsarchiv*, Düsseldorf. (Most of the Diplomatic archives of the Electorate of Cologne have been lost.)
Han.   *Niedersächsisches Staatsarchiv*, Hannover.
Marburg   Hessisches Staatsarchiv, Marburg.
PRO   Public Record Office.
RA   Royal Archives, Windsor.
Vienna   *Oesterreichisches Staatsarchiv*, Wien. (With one exception, all citations refer to the series 'England'.)
Wolfenbuttel *Niedersächsisches Staatsarchiv*, Wolfenbüttel.

Printed Manuscript sources

Aspinall, A. The later Correspondence of George III, Cambridge, 1962.
Frederick   *Politische Korrespondenz Friedrichs des Grossen*, Berlin, 1879.
Hist. MSSC   Historical Manuscripts Commission.
Sbornik   *Sbornik Imperatorskago Russkago Istoriceskago Obscestva*, St. Petersburg 1867-1916. (A collection of correspondence with the Imperial Russian court and the local embassies, much of it in the original — non-Russian — languages. To be found under 'Leningrad' in the British Library.)
Wellington   Despatches, Correspondence and Memoranda of Field Marshall Arthur Duke of Wellington. London, 1875.

186

Printed Books

Annual Register 1758-1838.

Allgemeine Deutsche Biographie, Leipzig, 1886 ff.

Ausführliche Relation . . . (George I's arrival in England), Leipzig, 1714.

Baasch, E., *Der Kampf des Hauses Braunschweig-Lüneburg mit Hamburg um die Elbe*, Leipzig, 1905.

Beattie, J.M., *The English Court in the Reign of George I*, Cambridge, 1967.

Belsham, W., *Memoirs of the Kings of Great Britain*, London, 1793.

Bicke and Kluxen (eds.), *England und Hannover — England and Hanover*, London, 1986.

Bingmann, K., *Das rechtliche Verhältnis zwischen Grossbritannien und Hannover von 1714-1837*, doctoral thesis, Würzburg, 1923.

Black, J., *Eighteenth Century Europe 1700-1789*, London, 1990.

Black, J., *The Rise of the European Powers 1679-1793*, London, 1990.

Brauer. G., *Die hannoversch-englischen Subsidienverträge 1702-1748*, doctoral thesis, Frankfurt, 1962.

Brandis, Schütz v.Brandis (ed. Frhr. v.Reitzenstein), *Uebersicht über die Geschichte der Hannoverschen Armee 1617-1866*, Leipzig, 1903.

Braubach, M., *Vom Westfälischen Frieden bis zur französischen Revolution*, Stuttgart, 1970.

Braubach, M., *Von der französischen Revolution bis zum Wiener Kongress*, Stuttgart, 1970.

Brooke, J., *George III*, Frogmore, 1974.

Brown, P.D. and Schweiger, K.W. (eds.), *The Devonshire Diary (1759-62)*, Royal Historical Society, London, 1982.

Bruford, W.H., *Germany in the 18th Century*, Cambridge, 1965.

Cambridge Modern History, vol. VI, Cambridge, 1909.

(New) Cambridge Modern History, vols. VII and IX, Cambridge, 1957, 1965.

Chance, J.F., *George I and the Northern War*, London, 1909.

Cipolla, C.M. (ed.), *The Fontana Economic History of Europe*, vols. 3 and 4, Glasgow, 1973.

Conrady, S., '*Die Wirksamkeit König Georgs III für die Hannoverschen Kurlande*', in: *Niedersächsisches Jahrbuch für Landesgeschichte*, vol. 39, 1967.

Cowper, *Diary of Lady Mary Cowper (1714-1720)*, London, 1864.

Coxe, W., *Memoirs of the Administration of Henry Pelham*, London, 1829.

Coxe, W., *Memoirs of the Life and Administration of Sir Robert Walpole*, London, 1798.

Curiosa Relaçam da Guerra entre . . . *França e Inglaterra*, Lisbon 1757 (a collection of official publications by the contending states in the Seven Years' War).

Dann, U., *Hannover und England 1740-1760*, Heidelberg, 1986.

Davies, J.D.G., *A King in toils*, London, 1938.

Devonshire Diary, see: Brown, P.D. and Schweiger, K.W.

Drögereit, R. '*Das Testament Georgs I und die Frage der Personalunion zwischen England und Hannover*', in: *Niedersächsisches Jahrbuch*, vol. 14, 1937.

England and Hanover, see: Bicke and Kluxen.

English Historical Documents, London, 1957.

Eldon, C.W., *England's subsidy policy towards the Continent during the Seven Years'*

War, Philadelphia, 1930.

Ellis, K.L., '*The administrative connection between Britain and Hanover*', in: *Journal of the Society of Archivists*, 1965-69.

Ford, G.S., *Hanover and Prussia 1795-1800*, New York, 1903.

Gehling, T., *Europäischer Diplomat am Kaiserhof zu Wien 1718-1727* (St. Saphorin), *Bonner historische Forschungen*, vol. 25.

Gentlemen's Magazine, 1750-1839.

Genzel, F., *Studien zur Geschichte des Nordischen Krieges 1714-1720 unter besonderer Berücksichtigung der Personalunion zwischen Hannover und Grossbritannien*, unprinted doctoral thesis, Bonn, 1951.

Gerhard, D., *England und der Aufstieg Russlands*, Berlin, 1933.

Grieser, R., 'Die Deutsche Kanzlei in London, ihre Entstehung und Anfänge', in: *Niedersächsische Blätter für Landesgeschichte*, vol. 89, 1952.

Gruner, W.D., 'England, Hannover und der Deutsche Bund' in *England and Hanover*, 1937.

Haase, C., 'Göttingen und Hannover', in: *Göttinger Jahrbuch 1967*, pp.95ff.

Hannoverscher Staatskalender, 1820.

Hassell, v., *Das Kurfürstentum Hannover vom Basler Frieden bis ... 1806*, Hannover, 1894.

Hassell, v., *Geschichte des Königreichs Hannover 1813-1848*, Bremen, 1898.

Hatton, R.M., *George I*, London, 1978.

Hatton, R.M., *Charles XII of Sweden*, London, 1968.

Hatton, R.M. and Bromley (eds), *William III and Louis XIV*, Liverpool, 1968.

Hatton, R.M., *The Anglo-Hanoverian Connection 1714-1760*, Creighton Trust Lecture, 1982.

Havemann, W., *Geschichte der Lande Braunschweig und Lüneburg*, vol. 2, Lüneburg, 1838.

Heinemann, O.v., *Geschichte von Braunschweig und Hannover*, vol. 3, Hannover, 1975.

Hervey, *Lord Hervey's Memoirs*, ed. R. Szednik, London, 1963.

Hibbert, C., *The Court at Windsor*, London, 1964.

Hibbert, C., *George IV*, London, 1972.

Hist. Mus., *Hannover im Glanz und Schatten des Britischen Weltreiches*, by W.R. Röhrbein and A. v.Rohr, published by the Historisches Museum Hannover, 1977.

Hunt, W. and Poole, L. (eds.), *The Political History of England*, London, 1906 (reprinted New York, 1969).

Jarrett, D., *Britain 1688-1815*, London, 1965.

Jones, J.R., *Britain and the World 1649-1815*, Glasgow, 1980.

King, P., *The Life of John Locke*, London, 1829.

König, T., *Hannover und das Reich 1740-1745*, doctoral thesis, Bonn, 1938.

Lecky, W.E.H., *A History of England in the Eighteenth Century*, London, 1892.

Leeds, *Political Memoranda of Francis, Fifth Duke of Leeds*, Camden Society 1884.

Lenthe, v., *Briefe des Ministers Otto Christian von Lenthe*, R. Grieser (ed.), Hildesheim, 1977.

Lodge, Sir R., *Great Britain and Prussia in the 18th Century*, Oxford, 1923.

Lodge, Sir R., *Studies in European Diplomacy 1740-1748*, London, 1930.

Mahon (Lord Mahon), *History of England 1713-1783*, London, 1853.

Marshall, D., *Eighteenth-Century England*, London, 1962.

Mediger, W., *Moskaus Weg nach Europa*, Braunschweig, 1957.

Mediger, W., *Mecklenburg, Russland und England-Hannover 1706-1724*, Hildesheim, 1967.

Meier, v., *Hannoversche Verfassungs- und Verwaltungsgeschichte 1686-1866*, Leipzig, 1898.

Melville, L., *The First George*, London, 1908.

Meyer, R., *Die Neutralitätsverhandlungen des Kurfürstentums Hannover beim Ausbruch des Siebenjährigen Krieges*, doctoral thesis, Kiel, 1912.

Michael, W., *Englische Geschichte im 18. Jahrhundert*, 5 vols., Hamburg and Leipzig, 1896-1955.

Mitchell, Sir A., *Memoirs and Papers*, A. Bisset (ed.), London, 1850.

Munster, G.H. Count, *Political Sketches of the State of Europe from 1814-1867*, Edinburgh, 1868.

Murray, J.J., *George I, the Baltic, and the Whig split of 1717*, London, 1969.

Namier, Sir L., *The Structure of Politics at the Accession of George III*, London, 1960.

Ompteda, L.Frhr. v., *Notizen eines deutschen Diplomaten (1804-1813)*, Berlin, 1935.

Ompteda, F.Frhr. v., *Die Ueberwältigung Hannovers durch die Franzosen*, Hannover, 1862.

Oestreich, G., *Verfassungsgeschichte vom Ende des Mittelalters bis zum Ende des alten Reiches*, Stuttgart, 1970.

Ogg, D., *Europe of the Ancien Regime*, London, 1965.

Owen, J.B., 'George II reconsidered', in: *Statesmen, Scholars, and Merchants*, Oxford, 1973.

Pares, R., *George III and the Politicians*, Oxford, 1967.

Parl. Hist., *The Parliamentary History of England 1016-1803*, Cobbett and Wright (eds.).

Pfannkuchen, A., *Die königlich deutsche Legion 1803-1806*, Hannover, 1926.

Plumb, J.H., *Sir Robert Walpole*, London, 1956.

Plumb, J.H., *The First Four Georges*, Fontana Library, 1966.

Portzek, H., *Friedrich der Grosse und Hannover in ihrem gegenseitigen Urteil*, Hildesheim, 1958.

Püster, K., *Möglichkeiten und Verfehlungen merkantilistischer Politik im Kurfürstentum Hannover unter Berücksichtigung des Einflusses der Personalunion mit dem Königreich Grossbritannien*, doctoral thesis, Hamburg, 1966.

Recueil des instructions aux ambassadeurs Français, vol. XVI.

Robertson, C.G., *England under the Hanoverians*, London, 1947.

Rose, J.H., 'Frederic the Great and England', in: *English Historical Review*, vol. 29, 1914.

Salomon. F., 'England und der deutsche Fürstenbund von 1785', in: *Historische Vierteljahresschrift*, vol. VI, 1903.

Schilling, H., *Der Zwist Preussens und Hannovers 1729/30*, Halle, 1912.

Schlenke, M., *England und das friederizianische Preussen 1740-1763*, Freiburg, 1963.

Schnath, G., *Geschichte Hannovers im Zeitalter der neunten Kur und der englischen Sukzession 1674-1704*, vol. IV, Hildesheim, 1982.

Sieske, G., *Preussen im Urteil Hannovers*, Hildesheim, 1953.

Storch, D., *Die Hannoversche Königskrone*, Hildesheim, 1982.

Trench, C.C., *George II*, London, 1975.

Treue, W., *Deutsche Geschichte von 1713 bis 1806*, Berlin, 1957.

Ulbricht, O., *Englische Landwirtschaft in Kurhannover in der zweiten Hälfte des 18. Jahrhunderts*, Berlin, 1980.

Williams, B., *The Whig Supremacy 1714-1760*, Oxford History of England, vol. XI.

Williams, B., *Stanhope*, Oxford, 1932.

Ward, A.W., *Great Britain and Hanover*, Oxford, 1899.

Wellington, *Despatches, Correspondence, and Memoranda of Field Marshall Arthur Duke of Wellington*, London, 1875.

Wersebe, W.v., *Geschichte der Hannoverschen Armee*, Hannover, 1928.

Willis, G.H., *Ernest Augustus, Duke of Cumberland and King of Hanover*, London, 1954.

Willis, G.H., *Ernst August, König von Hannover*, (not a translation), Hannover, 1961.

Yorke, P.C., *The Life and Correspondence of Philip Yorke, Earl of Hardwicke*, Cambridge, 1913.

Ziegler, P., *King William IV*, London, 1917.